The Benefits of Tax Competition

The Benefits of Tax Competition

RICHARD TEATHER

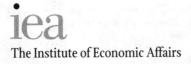

The Institute of Economic Affairs

First published in Great Britain in 2005 by
The Institute of Economic Affairs
2 Lord North Street
Westminster
London SW1P 3LB
in association with Profile Books Ltd

The mission of the Institute of Economic Affairs is to improve public understanding of the fundamental institutions of a free society, with particular reference to the role of markets in solving economic and social problems.

A CIP catalogue record for this book is available from the British Library.

ISBN 0 255 36569 1

Many IEA publications are translated into languages other than English or are reprinted. Permission to translate or to reprint should be sought from the Director General at the address above.

Typeset in Stone by MacGuru Ltd
info@macguru.org.uk
Printed and bound in Great Britain by Hobbs the Printers

CONTENTS

THE AUTHOR

Richard Teather is Senior Lecturer in Tax Law at Bournemouth University, one of the few UK universities to specialise in taxation law and policy. His teaching there includes specialised courses in international tax and in VAT, as well as the more standard business tax.

After reading law at Oxford, he qualified as a chartered accountant, acting as a tax adviser to a variety of businesses and their owners and managers, firstly in the global accounting firm Deloitte and then with Denton Wilde Sapte, a major international law firm based in the City of London. Much of his work involved a European or wider international angle, whether for UK companies expanding overseas or for foreign-based organisations setting up UK operations. He therefore has direct experience of the effect of taxes on cross-border business and investment.

He writes regularly on a range of tax issues, from highly technical matters to the morality of tax avoidance, and is a frequent speaker at conferences. He has been invited to lecture at universities across Europe, including in the ex-communist bloc as part of an EU programme to assist their transition to a market economy. Recently his work on tax reform has been debated in the UK Parliament, and he has defended his stance on radio.

FOREWORD

Governments often promote policies to curb the supposed power of monopolies, monopsonies and cartels. Sometimes, such policies are pursued because there is a technical understanding of the welfare losses that can arise from anti-competitive behaviour. But underlying such intervention there is often a general concern about the power that can be wielded by firms or groups of firms that subvert competition. There is often precious little understanding among governments that develop such policies about the true nature of competition and how open markets can undermine monopoly power without intervention – but that is another story.

Apparently without irony, politicians promote 'cooperation not competition' in the provision of government-provided services and regard 'tax competition' as harmful. Tax competition involves allowing sovereign nations, and dependencies with tax-setting powers, to set their own tax rates and rules. Impeding tax competition, through the operation of a cartel of governments that sets tax rates and/or rules, is an abuse of power by government, much more serious than any abuse by monopolies acting in private markets. It is more serious because governments have a monopoly of coercion and, if tax competition is prevented, individuals will be unable to choose the kind of governments under which they live or the kind of countries in which they invest on the basis of their preferences for different amounts of government-provided services. Tax cartels are also more serious because, while a monopolist in a product market is always under threat from potential entry to the market or from new innovations that reduce demand for the monopolist's product, there is no such analogy for investors or employees if governments get together and agree to exact a penal portion of all incomes. Furthermore, the very methods by which attacks on tax competition are enforced are an abuse of power too: for example, requiring banks to share confidential information with governments is sinister and abhorrent to all who believe in a free society.

In Hobart Paper 153, Richard Teather shows that the economic arguments that are used to support attacks on tax competition are intellectually threadbare. Theoretical arguments that suggest that public goods will be under-provided if competition leads to a decline in tax rates make heroic assumptions that are simply untenable. Indeed, public choice economics predicts that government services will be over-provided in one-person-one-vote democracies: tax competition can mitigate this effect. In fact, as Teather shows, most practices that are described by high-tax countries as 'harmful tax competition' are, in fact, designed to prevent the double or triple taxation of returns from capital that can arise as a result of different approaches to taxing investment income being followed in different countries.

As has been mentioned, the mechanisms used to prevent tax competition are draconian. The fear of governments is that the tax base will be whittled down and that governments will not be able to provide basic public services. The loudest voices expressing those fears are EU governments, which currently tax their citizens at a rate of between 40 and 65 per cent of their income. Such governments should not use less powerful nations as unpaid tax collectors and enforcers. They should set rates that are acceptable in a liberal society and enforce them themselves. But Teather also shows that the most harmful tax practices are actually undertaken by EU governments themselves. These do not involve generally low levels of taxes but, instead, special tax exemptions for certain types of economic activity. Some of these are outlawed by the European Commission but others are ignored. All these special tax exemptions lead to the same sort of welfare losses as arise from subsidising particular industries, and can be damaging to the development of free trade.

The author's case is persuasive. Attacks on tax competition from politicians and bureaucrats are self-serving and hypocritical. Yet tax competition is under threat from many quarters. If the opponents of tax competition are successful, they will undermine one of the few sources of downward pressure that can prevent the size of government from rising way above optimal levels. Attacks on tax competition will also put at risk certain fundamental aspects of a free society that liberals should treasure.

The views expressed in Hobart Paper 153 are, as in all IEA publications, those of the author and not those of the Institute (which has no corporate view), its managing trustees, Academic Advisory Council members or senior staff.

PHILIP BOOTH

Editorial and Programme Director,
Institute of Economic Affairs
Professor of Insurance and Risk Management,
Sir John Cass Business School, City University
November 2005

SUMMARY

- Tax competition is the process by which governments attempt to attract capital and labour to their country by offering low tax rates or other tax incentives.

- Tax competition brings great benefits, to all society and not just to those who directly take advantage of it. But the greatest benefits go to those countries that work in harmony with global free markets, not to those protectionists who try to erect barriers against the tide.

- The reduction in barriers to international trade, investment and relocation in the 1980s not only improved the operation of the global free market but also allowed more people to take advantage of low tax rates in other countries. It therefore made tax competition more effective, and helped prompt much-needed tax reform.

- Tax competition acts as a check on governments' ability to raise taxes; it ensures that governments have more limited funds and thus provides incentives for governments to spend more wisely.

- By preventing taxes becoming too high, tax competition boosts economic welfare, productive investment and employment. Low-tax jurisdictions also make global capital markets more efficient.

- These benefits, of more efficient government spending and

more productive capital investment by business, flow to everyone, not just to those who benefit directly from low-tax jurisdictions.

- Opposition to tax competition is misguided, being based either on a misunderstanding of tax havens (which do not capture investment but merely direct it to where it can be best used) or idealistic assumptions about government. In the real world, tax competition is beneficial.
- The current attempts by European governments (through the EU and the OECD) to restrict tax competition will therefore damage the world economy and harm their citizens. The UK and US governments should follow their belief in the benefits of the global free market and resist these moves.
- If there is damaging tax competition, it is found in the tax breaks to specific businesses offered by EU governments. The UK should continue the reforms of the 1980s, offering a simple tax system with low rates for all businesses.
- It is hypocritical for EU governments to defend their own, harmful, tax exemptions while attacking open low-tax jurisdictions. The UK, with its historic links to many low-tax jurisdictions, should support their 'level playing field' campaign for fair treatment from the EU and OECD.

TABLES

The Benefits of Tax Competition

The Economics of the Competition

1   INTRODUCTION

The global marketplace

Since the mid-1980s international trade and investment have grown remarkably. To give some idea of the scale of international markets, in its latest survey the Bank of International Settlements put the volume of foreign currency trading at US$1.2 trillion per day. We are moving towards a truly globalised marketplace.

This has brought great increases in wealth. In the developed world even the poor are unimaginably rich when compared with their predecessors.

Even the poor regions have benefited from globalisation. Also, unlike in the colonial era, modern global trading cannot be characterised as mere exploitation of resources by the rich.[1] Poorer countries have ready access to the marketplaces of the rich and globalisation involves voluntary exchange, for the benefit of all parties.

These benefits are not confined to the 'West', as globalisation creates better-paid jobs in poorer countries where often the only alternative has been subsistence agriculture. Indeed, what were once known as the industrialised nations have seen their manufacturing bases disappear to the newly industrialised Asia. Yet this gain

---

1   A characterisation that is not necessarily valid.

Table 1 **GDP per capita, constant 1990 $**

	1820	1870	1913	1950	1973	1998
USA	1,257	2,445	5,301	9,561	16,689	27,331
W. Europe	1,232	1,974	3,473	4,594	11,534	17,921
Japan	669	737	1,387	1,926	11,439	20,413
Asia excluding Japan	575	543	640	635	1,231	2,936
Africa	418	444	585	852	1,365	1,368

Source: Maddison (2003: Appendix A)

for the newly industrialised countries has not impoverished the old ones; the process has brought gains for all parties, and employment has continued to rise in the UK despite the demise of manufacturing. The global marketplace has allowed Adam Smith's theory of specialisation to be applied on a worldwide basis, so that while once impoverished countries are increasing their standard of living by becoming the world's factory, the developed nations have concentrated on higher-value services and increasingly the creation of intellectual property. This is not just a benefit for the rich, for their high-value-added services also create local spin-off employment.

A global capital market

Global free trade has therefore brought previously unimagined benefits to the whole world. And hand in hand with global free trade, allowing it to function properly, is the globalisation of capital markets. According to the IMF, cross-border investment has grown massively, increasing from a low point of little more than 1 per cent of GDP in the post-war years to 2.6 per cent in the 1990s.

This cross-border flow of capital has allowed the global free market to be a practical reality, providing the finance to allow the developing nations to build and equip the factories, and recently the technological powerhouses, that enable them to compete globally.

Objections to global free markets

There have been objections to these processes. Some Westerners appear to object to globalisation on the grounds that subsistence agriculture, and the consequent low life expectancy, is somehow nobler than producing goods for export. Fortunately this view, although it attracts attention, is not generally widespread. In a free market we are all free to choose our level of participation, but very few people choose to die young.

Even the recent publicity campaign against globalisation by the aid organisation Christian Aid could not actually find anything wrong with the global free market to attack. What it criticised was instead the attempts by European governments to prevent a free market: the agricultural subsidies to European producers; and the import tariffs that protect them from 'Third World' competition, though the characterisation of those protectionist devices as being part of the 'free trade' agenda was misconceived.[2]

Tariffs, subsidies and protectionism do indeed cause problems for developing countries, but the problems are a consequence of anti-market action by governments, not the free markets themselves. Similarly there are problems in some countries that participate in the global free market without being internally free themselves. Opinions are divided as to whether in practice this can best be solved by punitive sanctions or by allowing the market

---

2   The Christian Aid campaign likened free trade to tsunamis.

to slowly break down their oppression, but again the problem is not an excess of free trade but its restriction.

There are indeed injustices caused by lack of freedom, and it is right to act against them, but all too often they are used as cover for those groups who feel their position threatened by global free trade. There are many who fail to understand the advantages that a widened free market can bring, while their potential for loss is all too obvious. The most obvious manifestation of this is the unions' objections to free markets: they fear that their members' jobs will be lost, or that in order to keep them they will have to sacrifice their hard-won pay and conditions, and so they call for protectionism.

These restrictions on the global free market rely on government enforcement powers to be effective. Of course, it is always open to unions to lobby consumers to reject foreign imports, and the consumers are free to decide that there are non-monetary benefits to buying locally produced goods and services which outweigh the increased cost or lower quality. Such campaigns, however, generally have little effect; although consumers may feel sympathetic, when the choice is before them they prove unwilling to make what are effectively donations to domestic workers that may not even be in the long-run best interests of such workers.

Fortunately these calls for protectionism are generally unanswered; except in the agricultural sector, the World Trade Organization rules against tariffs, quotas and other obstacles to trade increasingly protect free markets (although the Bush steel protections were an alarming development from a supposedly pro-freedom administration).

Tax competition

Unfortunately there is a more dangerous threat to global free markets, where the government is at once the enforcer and the beneficiary of the restrictions.

Under exchange controls the transfer of funds out of a country, whether or not to a low-tax jurisdiction, was often illegal, and many taxpayers had no choice but to accept their government's impositions.

In contrast, as the wartime exchange controls began to be removed in 1979, money became free to flow through the international capital markets. This increased spread of the global market encouraged investors to choose the country as well as the sector in which to invest their capital, and so the tax rate became merely another expense, like brokers' fees, to be offset against the potential return when making investment decisions. Private and institutional investors, and also multinational companies considering where to site their next operational expansion, began to focus on after-tax returns when deciding where to invest, and so the use of tax havens (territories with little or no effective taxation) grew.

Some of the early tax havens were accidental, but governments soon realised that deliberate reductions in effective tax rates could attract foreign capital investment. This is what is known as 'tax competition'.

The late 1990s saw increased suspicion of this activity on the part of European governments (particularly the large high-tax countries of Germany, Italy and France). There was a particular fear among politicians that the free market in capital would transfer investment from high-tax to low-tax economies and therefore prevent governments from raising taxes (particularly on investment income), threatening the post-war welfare state. This was bolstered by the theory that tax competition would result in a 'race to the bottom': governments competing to attract foreign capital by lowering their taxes would be sucked into a spiral of competitive tax reductions that would result in investment income being tax-free.

As a result the core European governments have begun concerted campaigns against tax havens, seeking either to force them to raise taxes or to emasculate their tax-efficient status in other ways. This has taken place at various levels; within the European Union, on a wider plane through the close historical and constitutional ties that many tax havens have with EU members (particularly the UK), and on a global basis through supra-national organisations such as the Organisation for Economic Co-operation and Development (OECD) and the United Nations (UN).

The current situation is that these European governments are using all these avenues (and other less reputable ones) in an attempt to stamp out tax competition. Their motives are the same as those of all who protest against true global free markets: a tendency to worry more about risks than opportunities, a desire for the status quo, and a distrust of economic freedom.

2 THE BENEFITS OF TAX COMPETITION

Introduction

Tax competition is the use by governments of low effective tax rates to attract capital and business activity to their country. This is believed to have a two-stage effect on the world's tax systems:

- First, some pioneer countries will reduce their tax rates, or otherwise alter their tax systems to offer low effective tax rates (countries that lower their tax rates to very low or zero levels are commonly known as 'tax havens').
- Second, other countries could lower their own taxes in response to perceived or actual losses from this competition.

This tax competition has grown as part of the general increase in international trade and investment, and is part of the process of globalisation. The opinion across the governments of most of the world's richest countries, however, is that it is bad and must be stamped out, and they are using various bodies (the EU, the OECD and the UN) in attempts to bring this about.

Is tax competition really damaging, or is it rather a force for good? There are three main areas where tax competition, and tax havens in general, affect the economy: they can have an impact on markets, on companies and also on governments.

Impact on markets – lower taxes mean greater wealth

Perhaps the most obvious result of tax competition is its beneficial impact on savings rates. High taxes (particularly high taxes on investment returns) tend to act as a disincentive to savings, so reducing the pool of available investment capital and therefore slowing growth and possibly leading to fewer jobs being created. If tax competition can keep tax rates down, particularly those on highly mobile investment capital, and so increase savings, then it will boost overall wealth.

Higher taxes on investment returns (whether the underlying business profits or the dividends and capital gains received by the investor) result in lower post-tax returns. The decision to save income rather than spend is based on the expectation that investment growth enables saving to result in higher spending in the future, and so high levels of taxation on investment returns reduce the chance of saving being beneficial (as does inflation, also primarily caused by governments).

Higher taxes on business profits also reduce investment in a more direct way; much investment is funded by way of companies' retention of their own profits to fund future business growth, and higher taxes on business profits leave less capital for this purpose. In addition, if investment income of the company's shareholders is being taxed highly then, in a competitive international capital market, companies may find that they have to pay out higher dividends to their shareholders in order to attract capital. This combination of lower post-tax profits for the company and higher dividend payouts can put a squeeze on retained earnings and damages expansion.

There is also a wider sense in which taxation, including tax on labour, damages economic growth. Work and other economic activity is a combination of costs and benefits: the difficulty of doing a job and the leisure time that is sacrificed is compared with the salary and other rewards. High tax rates shift the balance and make paid work less attractive. This drives a 'tax wedge' between the benefits that flow from work for the employer/client and those that can be transmitted to the worker, reducing work incentives and also undermining specialisation. With high levels of tax, the gains from following a paid occupation need to be much higher before it is worth following a paid occupation rather than subsistence 'do it yourself' (see Arthur, 2003, for a highly readable exposition of this).

Some of these effects depend on the specific tax system. Progressive tax systems, with higher tax rates on higher incomes, make difficult or stressful jobs less attractive by reducing the compensatory salaries. High taxes also risk a 'brain drain', the exodus of talented individuals to lower-taxed countries which was a widely observed phenomenon in the high-tax climate of the UK in the 1960s and 1970s. This is not just a problem for high earners, however. All tax systems also damage the less well off; low-productivity jobs are very marginal, with the value of the product to the employer little more than the cost of employment, and so even a small 'tax wedge' can make a job non-viable.

This effect is likely to be even more marked in the case of entrepreneurship. A business start-up involves significant risk in return for the hope of substantial rewards; high taxes reduce the value of the potential rewards but there is never a fully compensatory reduction in the risk, so making entrepreneurship (and even expansions for existing businesses) less attractive. This could be avoided by having fully symmetrical tax relief for losses, but in practice tax systems put restrictions on the ability to claim relief (for example, in the UK, unless one has substantial other income, tax relief for business losses can be obtained only by offsetting losses against profits in the previous year or in future years, which delays or, if the business folds before returning to profit, denies relief).

For all these reasons, high taxes reduce economic growth. This then affects the whole of society, because lower growth leads to fewer jobs, and so higher unemployment and lower net wages (as there is less competition among employers for labour). Indeed, workers are one of the main beneficiaries of economic growth; as demand for labour rises, firms have to compete for workers and so offer higher wages and improved conditions.

This effect of high taxes on economic growth is not accepted by all parties, and there are also counter-effects whereby high taxes can stimulate growth. It is argued that high taxes encourage more effort, as a greater pre-tax income is needed to maintain standards of living. There is also the possibility that high taxes will lead to government spending that boosts growth. This is possible where governments can provide certain valuable services and sometimes infrastructure at an efficient cost, but the profit motive and the price mechanism mean that the private sector is generally more likely to do this effectively across most goods and services.

Various studies have attempted to quantify the effects of taxes on economic growth, but it is difficult to isolate the impact of taxes from other factors. The predominant view of these studies, however, is that there is a link. Bassanini and Scarpetta (2001) for the OECD found that an extra 1 per cent of GDP taken in taxes would reduce economic growth by around 0.6 per cent. Other studies show lower amounts, but tend to agree on the principle that higher taxes reduce growth.

Table 2 **Growth rates in selected regimes (per cent)**

Country	Tax (% GDP) 1992	Tax (% GDP) 2002	Growth 1992–2002
Ireland	34	30	82
New Zealand	36	35	36
UK	35	38	28
France	43	45	21

Source: Leach (2003)

Although small, the cumulative effect of this reduction in growth over a few years can be significant. Unfortunately this loss is invisible; although it can lead to job losses, generally the problem manifests itself in the form of jobs that are never created.

As an example of the connection between high taxes and reduced economic growth, a survey by Leach (2003) examined the major industrialised economies over the previous decade. He found that over a ten-year period those countries with low or reducing taxes invariably had significantly stronger growth rates than those with high or increasing taxes. A few typical examples are shown in Table 2.

For a more extreme example, Bartholomew (2004) quotes figures (ultimately derived from Maddison's masterly millennial study for the OECD) comparing economic growth in the UK and Hong Kong. Although technically governed by the UK, the colonial government in Hong Kong had enough independence (and sense) to resist following the UK's tax rises in the 1960s and 1970s. As a result the UK reached a basic rate tax of 35 per cent and a top rate of 98 per cent in the 1970s, but Hong Kong kept a single rate of 15 per cent (and high allowances). The relative economic growth of the two jurisdictions is remarkable:

Table 3 **The UK and Hong Kong: GDP per capita, constant 1990 $**

	1950	1973	1999
UK	6,907	12,022	19,030
Hong Kong	2,218	7,104	20,352

Source: Maddison (2003) via Bartholomew (2004)

Hong Kong's growth in GDP per capita (800 per cent over the period as opposed to the UK's 175 per cent) is even more remarkable when you take account of its enormous inflow of impoverished refugees from the Chinese revolution (quintupling its population and putting a severe strain on infrastructure). It is a remarkable example of how a low-tax entrepreneurial economy can grow. Similar results have been seen in Estonia recently: the short-term job losses caused by post-communist reconstruction were countered with heavy tax cuts (and simplification), resulting in strong growth in new business start-ups.

Impact on markets – efficient global capital markets

The OECD, while recognising the benefits to the world economy of tax reductions (particularly those since the 1970s), thinks that tax havens cause distortions in the global capital market by attracting disproportionate levels of investment to themselves.

On the face of it this seems obvious, but it is true only on a simplistic level. Investors do indeed put a great deal of money into banks and other financial institutions in tax havens, and multinational groups channel part of their profits there, but that money does not stay in the traditional tax havens because they do not generally have much local industry in which it can be invested. Traditional tax havens are generally small, remote islands, with little opportunity for large-scale economic activity, so the money has to be reinvested back into companies in the industrialised countries – primarily the OECD members.

In other words the tax havens do not poach more than their fair share of international capital, they merely act as conduits for investment back into the industrialised countries.

This conduit action is necessary because tax systems do not cope very well with international investment. For a collective investment fund (such as a unit trust or mutual fund), there are three levels at which the investment could be taxed: when *companies* in which the fund invests make profits or pay dividends; when the *fund* receives dividends or makes a profit from selling shares; and when the *investors* receive their payments from the fund. If all this happens within the same country the tax system usually has rules to make sure that the money is taxed only once. Unfortunately countries have different tax systems, so if the investors are in different countries then the money can be taxed three times: three lots of tax at 40 per cent would leave little point in investing (even if each successive country taxes only the net amount received after tax from the one below, the cumulative effect of three layers of 40 per cent tax leaves only 21.6 per cent of the original amount).

This problem has been recognised, and the OECD has attempted to address it. As a result there are 'tax treaties' between countries which try to prevent this double taxation, but they are cumbersome and so generally insist that the investor owns 10–20 per cent of the company before they can be used; this may be fine for multinational corporate groups but is not much help to private investors.

This is where the tax havens help; if the fund is based in a tax haven then there can be at most two lots of tax (levied on the company in which the investment takes place, and on the investor) rather than three; admittedly this is not ideal, but at least it usually reduces the problem to a manageable level.

Tax haven jurisdictions are therefore clearly a valuable tool in the global capital market, at least at the current state of development, with a highly imperfect international system for the prevention of double taxation. By providing such an environment the havens make international capital markets more efficient and in many cases make international pooling of capital possible when it would otherwise be prevented by a lack of coordination of cross-border tax and investment regulations. By doing this they increase the amount of available international investment capital, and enable it to be invested down into the most profitable companies, whatever countries they are in, without distortions caused by the need to avoid double taxation.

By increasing the efficiency of global capital markets, and ensuring that funds can flow to the most appropriate investments, tax havens therefore increase the efficiency of the allocation of capital and, in turn, increase the global standard of living. In this way the tax havens benefit us all, whether or not we personally invest through them; indeed, as proper investment supports long-term valuable employment, tax havens give indirect benefits even to those workers who have no investments at all.

The OECD is, of course, ideally placed to help remove these barriers to international investment; an extension of double tax treaties, or even an international consensus on how collective investment funds are to be taxed, would do much to help reduce these problems of cross-border investment and make the use of tax havens less necessary. It is admittedly not an easy solution, as countries tend to have embedded approaches to such issues, but it is the type of agreement that the OECD has had success with in the past through its model tax treaty and the commentary thereon. Unfortunately the OECD now appears to be locked into its confrontational 'harmful tax practices' initiative rather than adopting an enabling approach.

Impact on business

If global capital markets are made more efficient by tax competition, this has a knock-on effect in forcing business to be more efficient.

We have seen that, by allowing investors to invest in other countries without the punitive taxation that often arises, perhaps unintentionally, as a result of the multiple taxation of investments, tax havens not only give investors a wider choice of where to put their money but also allow capital to move more easily between different countries. This has helped developing nations, which do not have enough indigenous capital and so have to rely on foreign capital, but has also forced all large companies to improve. Companies in the past could be very inefficient, because exchange controls meant that investors in their country had little choice where to invest. But as international capital markets developed, the incompetent corporate dinosaurs of the 1970s found that they no longer had that trapped pool of investors and had to improve if they were to continue to attract capital to finance their business operations.

Instead of relying on a captive national pool of capital for investment, business now has to compete in the global capital markets. This means that only the most efficient operations will be able to offer high enough returns to attract capital, and therefore businesses will be forced to reduce inefficiencies in order to survive.

Although these efficiency gains can lead to some short-term employment problems, in the medium term the drive for increased efficiency is beneficial for all parties. Not only do consumers benefit from lower prices, but also employment in an efficient operation adds more value and will therefore in the long term be more profitable and secure. The expansion of the domestic economy in this way is the best long-term guarantor of employee wealth.

Impact on governments
Restraint

Similarly, tax competition also affects the behaviour of governments. Supporters of the free market should recognise that tax competition is beneficial, just as other forms of competition are beneficial. It is competition which forces suppliers to provide the public with the goods and services that they require, and to pursue the efficiencies that let them do so at the right price. In the absence of competition, monopoly suppliers have less incentive to be efficient, and less need to provide what consumers want.

This is generally accepted when applied to commercial situations, but should be equally obvious in the case of governments. The government is, within its borders, the ultimate monopoly supplier, and even has coercive powers to force us to pay for its services whether or not we want them or even use them.

... in public work, as distinguished from private work,

there is no test of service. If private work is bad, private persons decline to have it. The test of competition, the freedom of choice, the checks on extravagance, and the incentives to betterment, which are essential elements of private business, are absent in dealings with a public body. Benn (1925)

As a monopoly supplier, government is therefore expected to be naturally inefficient and to have an inbuilt tendency to increase its costs and activities, and therefore increase taxation. There are, of course, other constraints on governments, such as the threat of revolution or total economic collapse, but these are crude weapons, harming the taxpayer and society through the loss of activity and investment as much as they harm the government through the loss of tax revenues. In contrast tax competition allows taxpayers (whether investor, company or worker) to move to a country with a more congenial tax system, rather than damaging themselves by simply withdrawing their labour or investment.

Efficiency

If tax competition acts as a restraint on governments' ability to raise taxes, then it should also act as a spur to greater efficiency in the public sector. Governments will be faced with not only electoral demands for improvements in public services, or transfer payments to client groups, but also the countervailing pressure of tax competition restricting their ability to increase revenues by raising taxes. The only way to resolve this is to make better use of the limited resources available.

This increased efficiency is not only about how governments

carry on their activities; much more important often is what activities they choose to undertake. Modern representative governments have a tendency to be unduly influenced by vocal minority pressure groups, or by the need for politicians to satisfy their client groups in the electorate or their party (or even by their own desire for publicity, as in the case of Olympic Games bids), which means that public funds are often spent on projects that are not sufficiently valued by the population.[1]

The fact that government is inefficient now appears to be accepted by all political parties, at least in the UK. In the 2005 election Labour and the Conservatives competed to identify greater savings in bureaucracy, whereby costs could be reduced while still increasing output value. Whether any concrete improvements are made is more a matter of political will and organisational ability, but at least the principle has been established. There seems, however, to be a strong public sector inertia against such reforms (see Parkinson, 1958), so tax competition has an important role in giving the government an incentive to act and to keep the brake on further growth of waste.

Conclusion

The benefits of tax competition have been visible for the last twenty years; the post-war climate of high taxation was coupled with insularity and strong controls on emigration of capital and business. As controls were swept away, allowing people and investment funds to move more readily again, governments once again faced the possibility of a flight of money, investment and

---

1   See the public choice economics literature, summarised in Tullock et al. (2000).

(to some extent) people. Furthermore, in an increasingly multinational economy it was necessary for a country not only to retain its own people and capital but also to attract people and capital from abroad.[2]

These changes, and this need to be competitive internationally in the face of tax competition, forced governments to adopt more internationally competitive taxation systems and hence more efficient and streamlined government operations. The era of free international capital markets and the increased tax competition that these allowed led to the public finance reforms of the 1980s and 1990s. In the UK this was most visible in the Howe/Lawson reforms of the 1980s; punitive taxation of investment returns was ended, and for companies a system of high tax rates but a narrow tax base was replaced by a more business-friendly approach of low rates applied to a broad tax base roughly in line with accounting profits, which removed many perverse incentives.

Even the OECD admits these benefits:

> The more open and competitive environment of the last decades has had many positive effects on tax systems, including the reduction of tax rates and broadening of tax bases which have characterized tax reforms over the last 15 years. In part these developments can be seen as a result of competitive forces that have encouraged countries to make their tax systems more attractive to investors. In addition to lowering overall tax rates, a competitive environment can promote greater efficiency in government expenditure programs. (OECD 2001a)

---

2   This may sound like a 'zero sum game' but, as any economist should recognise, it is not. If capital is attracted from people living in a country where returns to capital are low, both the receiving country and the investors in the capital-exporting country benefit.

3 ECONOMIC ANALYSIS OF TAX COMPETITION

Introduction

As global capital markets developed and tax competition became strengthened, it began to attract academic study, particularly from economists.

Assuming that tax competition works, and it does appear to have a genuine impact, it is still valid to question whether it is truly beneficial or harmful. Numerous studies have been made of the harm or otherwise of tax competition, most concluding that it is damaging, but these are generally coloured by their underlying assumptions.

Three strands of study have emerged as the debate has evolved. Initial, somewhat uncritical, studies began with a general analysis of tax competition based on Tiebout's study of local authority spending decisions (Tiebout, 1956). Later, more complex algebraic models based on Samuelson's theory of efficient public goods (see below) saw tax competition as a harmful 'race to the bottom' which would result in inefficient allocation of resources and under-taxation as governments competed to attract capital. Finally the debate has widened, as scholars begin to question the assumptions on which previous studies were based, and tax competition is seen as being, in the real world, a beneficial part of global capital efficiency.

Tiebout's 1956 study saw competing local governments as providing different packages of services, which would attract different households based on their individual preferences. This resulted in a positive view of inter-governmental competition, allowing different preferences to be met across a state through variety in devolved government. The attempts by some governments to bring about international tax harmonisation, with minimum levels of tax imposed in all countries, would lose these Tiebout preference benefits.

Subsequent studies criticised the Tiebout-based models for being simplistic, particularly for their underlying assumptions ('it is often assumed that each region's government is controlled by its landowners, who seek to maximise the after-tax value of the region's land by attracting individuals to reside on this land' (Wilson, 1999); it is not surprising that a model that seems to be based on a caricature of the UK before the 1832 Reform Act has been attacked as being simplistic).

Unfortunately the next line of studies, although superficially more complex, is based on an equally unrealistic set of assumptions.

In the mid-1980s there were several attempts to model this interaction between different territories with a focus on the externality effects of tax competition in order to show its harmful nature (see Zodrow and Mieszkowski, 1986; Wilson, 1986).

Much of the political objection to tax competition is based on this externality argument, that the territory under examination may improve the overall welfare of its residents by engaging in tax competition, but by doing so it reduces the welfare of residents of other territories. This comes from comparing states not subject to tax competition with those that are. Governments, the theory says, raise taxes and spend them on the provision of public goods (i.e. benefits to the population at large that cannot be provided by the market). Without tax competition, Samuelson's rule of public goods provision says that governments will raise taxes as long as the benefits that flow from the public spending are greater than the cost, but no farther. At that point there is said to be perfect economic efficiency, as all profitable but no unprofitable public expenditure has been carried out.

This is illustrated by the formula $MB = MC$: marginal benefit (the advantages of an extra pound of government expenditure) is exactly equal to its marginal cost. If taxes or public spending are increased beyond this point then $MB < MC$: the benefit of the extra spending is less than the tax cost. If spending drops below this level then there is a welfare loss because projects where $MB > MC$ are not being undertaken and so the population has lost the benefit of profitable government expenditure.

There is, therefore, in the absence of tax competition, supposedly an economically efficient equilibrium; all countries will raise taxes to provide public services where the benefits are greater than the costs, but no farther.

The studies then contrast this with the situation where tax competition exists. If a government is considering raising additional taxes to fund proposed public expenditure, then it will again compare the benefits that will flow from this expenditure with the costs. When there is tax competition, however, there is not just the direct cost of the expenditure but also an indirect cost due to capital fleeing the country to lower-taxed jurisdictions.[1] In order to be beneficial for that country's residents, there-

---

1   In fact some studies assume that capital is immobile, and that the effect of a tax increase is to lower wages so that overall post-tax returns on capital remain the same. The principle is unchanged, however; they see an overall negative effect on

fore, the proposed government expenditure has to satisfy the test $MB = MC + X$; the benefits must be enough to cover not only the direct costs but also 'X', the indirect loss to the national economy caused by tax competition resulting in an outflow of capital to lower-taxed countries.[2]

At first sight this seems to be merely a better application of Samuelson, in that public spending decisions are made by including the indirect as well as the direct costs of taxation. Under these studies, however, it is assumed that on a global level there is no cost 'X'; global capital is assumed to be constant, and one country's loss is merely another's gain (matching positive and negative externalities). On this basis, looking at the global economy as a whole, there is under-spending on public goods because individual national governments are setting too high a hurdle in testing whether or not additional public spending (and associated taxes) are beneficial. There is therefore potential public expenditure that, if looked at on a global level, would be beneficial because $MB > MC$, but when looked at on a national level is rejected because $MB < MC + X$.

These studies therefore conclude that international tax harmonisation at a global level would be beneficial. On a global level there would be no loss of capital (because global capital is assumed to be fixed), and therefore X could be ignored, and all profitable public expenditure (where $MB > MC$) would be approved.

---

national welfare whether due to capital flight or reduced wages.

2   'X' is used here to stand for what is generally a more complex value that varies between different studies, but the effect, that there is an addition to marginal cost, is the same. The value of X will of course depend on a number of factors, particularly the mobility of capital; land is of course immobile, and the mobility of financial capital was for a time restricted by exchange controls or capital export restrictions.

Game theory and the race to the bottom

The algebraic studies of tax competition were taken farther by using Nash's game theory to examine the action of governments. If there is tax competition then an individual government can increase its subjects' welfare at the expense of other countries by reducing taxes and public spending so far as the loss of benefit from not undertaking worthwhile government expenditure is balanced by the national benefit from low taxes attracting a greater share of global capital (i.e. from the point where MB = MC to the point where MB = MC + X).

This is not a stable equilibrium, however. If country A does this then it is possible for the government of country B to respond in the same manner, reducing its public spending and attracting capital from country A. This will reduce welfare in country A, which can then respond again by reducing its government expenditure to attract back some of the mobile capital.

At each stage the country that reduces its government spending increases its own wealth at the expense of the other country, but also at an overall loss to the global economy (because profitable public expenditure is not being undertaken, the gain to the country that reduces its taxes is less than the loss to the other country). Over the course of several rounds of reduction, both countries would lose because the lost net marginal benefit from failing to undertake worthwhile public sector programmes means that the gains on their own tax reductions would not compensate for the losses when the other country responds.

This is the origin of the 'race to the bottom' that features heavily in political objections to tax competition. If the process is followed through to its logical conclusion, then eventually taxes will fall to zero because at each reduction there is an advantage to the country that makes it. Only if countries cooperate can this be avoided, because international coordination will take account of the overall losses.

Recent developments

There have been some attempts to fine-tune these theories. Wilson (1991) looks at the effect of different-sized countries, and concludes that effectively X is larger for small countries than it is for larger ones (because small economies can gain a relatively large advantage by attracting a relatively small proportion of global capital), and so a reduction in public expenditure is likely to be beneficial for small countries (because the benefits of the capital inflow will be relatively large), but not for large countries (where the capital inflow relative to the size of their economy will be less, and therefore may not outweigh the loss caused by the reduced public expenditure).

Baldwin and Forslid (2002) point out a curious anomaly: the opponents of tax competition assume that public spending is valuable, but also assume that mobile tax bases do not value it. The studies all assume that tax is the only factor taken into account when planning where to invest, site a factory or move to work. In fact the research suggests that tax rates are only one factor in a company's decision about where to invest, and that infrastructure, access to markets and workforce skills are also important (Ruding, 1992, surveyed nearly a thousand companies to conclude that tax was only one of a range of factors affecting location decision, and that tax was comparatively less important in the location of physical plant than of purely financial invest-ments). If some of these factors can be provided efficiently by government, then investment could actually flow to a country that taxes capital to fund these other factors rather than a zero-tax jurisdiction. Indeed, if one considers the core functions of government (defence, internal security, ensuring the security of property rights and the enforcement of contracts), these public services are vital for business to thrive.

One of the more interesting studies (Boadway et al., 1999) used game theory to look at the alternative to tax competition for states, and concluded that, if deprived of the ability to compete for international capital on tax grounds, states will instead compete by slashing welfare payments to reduce labour costs (there are wider issues of regulatory competition between governments which raise similar arguments to those of tax competition). Even this study, however, claims that tax competition is damaging, just not as damaging as the alternative. All these studies suffer from the same problem: they are based on unreasonable assumptions that oversimplify the global economy.

Problems with theories of tax competition

The most easily observed problem with these theories of tax competition is of course that their predicted outcome, that countries will engage in competitive reductions in their tax rates until they settle at little above zero, has not come about. There do seem to have been some effects of tax competition, possibly a slowing of the increase in tax rates and more likely a slight shift from taxation of capital to labour (which is thought to be less mobile and therefore produces a less effective form of tax competition), but overall average European tax rates are still around 45 per cent (EU (Eurostat), 2004). There have been occasional attempts to reconcile the theory with reality (see Wilson, above), but much of the debate has remained theoretical.

One error in the studies is that they take account only of the positive net benefit of public, not private, expenditure. It is true that if MB > MC for a public expenditure project then there will be a net increase in wealth. This fails, however, to take account of opportunity costs; it may well be that there is private expenditure (including investment) that could have been undertaken where the net benefit (MB–MC) is greater than for the proposed public expenditure. The public expenditure may therefore increase wealth when compared with doing nothing, but might not when compared with the possible private sector use of the same funds had they not been taken in taxation.

Johnsson (2004) has studied this from the Swedish perspective. Wealth is caused by a division of labour (Ricardo's comparative advantage; Adam Smith's match factory), where instead of doing everything for ourselves we each work at what we do best and pay others to do what they do best for us, creating voluntary mutual cooperation. Tax drives a wedge through this, because our income from work is taxed, which leaves us with less to spend on the services of others. It may therefore be more efficient for me to stay at home and mow my own lawn than to go out to work (the proceeds of which will be taxed) and pay a gardener (who needs higher gross pay because he will be taxed as well). The result of tax is therefore a reduction in productive economic activity, an unemployed gardener and poorly cut grass.

False assumptions in the tax competition literature

But these are minor errors. The fundamental problem with the algebraic (including Nash-based) models of tax competition is that in order to derive workable formulae they have to be simplified. In doing so, all the studies have to make assumptions that are not in accordance with the real world. Whether because of political bias or merely out of a need for simplicity, these assumptions tend to mean that the algebraic models of tax competition ignore the problems of governments that tax competition can solve. It is not surprising that if they ignore the potential benefits of tax competition they conclude that it must be harmful.

Global capital is fixed

Almost all the economic studies of tax competition assume that the total amount of global capital is fixed, and operate on the basis that the only effect of taxation on capital is its location, not the total amount. In some cases this is a fundamental assumption; in others it flows from underlying assumptions. Boadway et al. (1999), for example, assume that the number of active entrepreneurs in the economy is a constant, despite the wide debate on the effect of taxation policies on the number of business start-ups. Others take land (which is necessarily fixed in total, though the amount in productive use is not fixed) as being the only form of capital. The assumption, however, whether explicit or implicit, is always present.

The studies therefore ignore the beneficial effects of reduced taxes in encouraging saving and therefore increasing the available pool of capital. This has already been discussed at length, and although there is disagreement as to the precise magnitude of this effect (see Leach, 2003, for an overview of recent studies) there is little reasonable doubt that it exists.

The economic studies therefore ignore one of the main benefits of tax competition: by lowering tax rates the total amount of global capital, and therefore global wealth, is increased. Unfortunately, in most studies of tax competition economics is seen as a simplistic matter of dividing the cake, rather than encouraging it to grow.

The same approach can equally be applied to tax competition in other areas, such as labour, where the reduced marginal rates of tax encouraged by tax competition can increase global wealth by stimulating effort or reducing the 'tax wedge' (the gap between the cost an employer has to pay and the after-tax amount that an employee receives, which can stop marginal jobs from being financially worthwhile). A reduced tax wedge can increase wealth by improving employment rates and labour market participation.

Global capital markets are unaffected by tax systems

Similarly, the studies also assume that the only effect of tax on global capital markets is to direct investment to lower-taxed economies. As part of this there is generally the assumption that a single tax system (generally a very simplistic one) operates in all countries, with only the rates being different. As explained above, lack of congruity between national tax systems can often operate as a barrier to free capital markets, and can discourage cross-border investment. Tax havens can act as a partial solution to this problem, and so can make global capital markets more efficient, directing investment to the most appropriate place irrespective of tax considerations, and so increasing global wealth.

Government spending is perfectly efficient

The models assume that government expenditure is perfectly efficient so long as all potential projects where the benefit is greater than the cost are carried out (Samuelson's equilibrium where MB = MC). This is merely a theoretical efficiency, however, not a practical one; it assumes that for any proposed government expenditure there is a fixed benefit (MB) that can be obtained at a fixed cost (MC). It therefore ignores the fact that a proposed project has to be carried out in the real world, where costs can be increased by practical inefficiencies and reduced by practical efficiencies.

The assumption throughout most of the tax competition debate is that taxation is transformed into the provision of public goods without loss or waste. A few writers have attempted to deal with this, concluding that without this assumption the effect of tax competition on public welfare is 'ambiguous' (Boss, 1999) because a proportion of the benefits of taxation are lost through 'waste and inefficiencies in the public sector', but their work is generally dismissed by other writers owing to lack of quantification. It seems that it is always better to build a mathematical claim on false assumptions than to suggest unquantifiable truths.

In reality monopoly suppliers have no incentive to be efficient, and little need to provide what the consumers want, and so the government, as the ultimate monopoly supplier (its monopoly position is protected by law, unlike that of most monopolists), is naturally inefficient. The idea of practical inefficiencies in government does not depend on lack of goodwill or particular ineptitude on the part of the government and its employees. Rather it recognises that practical inefficiencies, the growth of bureaucracies and waste are a naturally occurring phenomenon (Parkinson) that takes effort to counter. This effort will be strong enough to overcome the inertia of inefficiency only where there is a sufficiently strong incentive; in the private sector this incentive is provided by the conflict between the demands of shareholders for higher profits and those of customers for lower prices. The democratic process ought to provide a certain incentive, but this is weak (particularly where there is a substantial electoral group who are net beneficiaries of government services).

If governments are not perfectly efficient (in a practical sense), then it is possible for government expenditure to be at a technically efficient equilibrium, where MB = MC for a given value of MB and MC, but for there still to be practical inefficiencies so that the same total benefits could be obtained at a lower cost. If these practical efficiencies were realised, then (all other things being equal) the economy would settle at a new equilibrium, where $MB_2 = MC_2$, at which point the increased practical efficiencies would ensure that the total benefits of government spending would be greater and the total expenditure less (effectively the government expenditure curve is shifted).

As discussed above, one of the advantages of tax competition is that it gives an incentive for governments to act efficiently. This is also accepted in the Tiebout models, and is the basis of their claim that tax competition is beneficial, and although the Tiebout line of analysis can be criticised for oversimplification this is a charge that can be levied equally well at its critics. The arithmetic models do not overturn the Tiebout model but rather ignore it, by assuming that governments without tax competition would be perfectly efficient, and therefore ignore one of the advantages of tax competition that should be set against any disadvantages.

Governments are perfectly benevolent and knowledgeable

As has been shown, the 1980s studies largely resulted in the conclusion that tax competition is inefficient (e.g. Janeba and Schjelderup, 2004), distortionary, inequitable or generally welfare-reducing (see Gorter and Mooij, 2001, for a comprehensive overview), as it leads to reduced revenues for governments and therefore reduced welfare spending.

The foundation of the Samuelson theory of public good provision, and the theories of tax competition that rest on it, is that governments raise taxes and fund expenditure up to the point where $MB = MC$. If governments spend money on provisions that are not desired or valued by their citizens, however, where for the population as a whole $MB < MC$, then all these studies fail because there is no natural state of bliss where, in the absence of tax competition, governments are perfectly efficient.

This false assumption flows from another fundamental misconception in these studies of tax competition: the belief that governments are perfectly benevolent and knowledgeable, and therefore spend money only for the provision of public goods (which cannot be provided efficiently by the market) that are valued by the population at large. This is sometimes explicitly assumed, but is more often implicit in the assumption that public spending automatically and necessarily equals public benefit and that government revenues automatically result in spending on projects that increase public welfare. The OECD's work also makes this assumption; the 1998 report refers throughout to loss of tax revenue for governments, but the implication is that this equates to a loss of welfare for their citizens.

Sometimes this assumption is indirect, flowing from other assumptions. Many of the studies claim that all citizens are homogeneous, so that their needs and wants are the same. As part of this, some state that capital is equally divided among citizens. Some attempt to be more realistic, saying that 'levels of taxation and public goods provision within jurisdictions are settled by majority voting' and that therefore overall government expenditure is likely to be benevolent (Perroni and Scharf, 1996). All these, however, ignore the reality of modern politics, that electorates are diverse and contain groups with different desires, and that they are affected by government politics in different ways.

In practice, in modern electorates the group that controls productive capital is a small minority.[3] Of course, workers are also adversely affected by taxes on capital, as they reduce investment and therefore the prospect of higher-wage, value-added jobs, but many find this link to be counter-intuitive.

Are governments only beneficial? Is potential public spending actually subjected to the test that MB > MC for the population as a whole? If not, then there is another source of advantage for tax competition, in that it can force governments to direct their spending to projects that will be valued most by their electorate. In effect tax competition would therefore provide an incentive for governments to act as if they were benevolent, just as it also gives them an incentive to act efficiently in the practical sense. If governments are not perfectly benevolent, then they will not necessarily judge potential expenditure on the basis that MB > MC, or at least the marginal benefit that they use will not be the benefit to the population at large, but to some other group (either the governing

3   The group of beneficial owners of capital may be much larger, but in general this is held through pension funds and other indirect methods; not only are these generally too indirect to give the owners the feeling that they are affected by taxes on capital, in practice they are frequently not affected because they are tax exempt.

group themselves, or their client groups in the electorate). If they are not perfectly knowledgeable, then they will use incorrect values for MB and MC, and therefore make wasteful spending decisions.

Elected governments come into power by building a coalition of support from within the electorate, and therefore there is an incentive to increase taxes on the minority to pay for benefits for client groups within the electorate. For example, if taxable capital is concentrated in the hands of a minority, with the majority being workers with no investments, then the government can (at least initially) raise taxes on capital without losing majority support. The proceeds of these taxes can then be spent on public services; even if MB < MC for the population as a whole, the political calculus will still be satisfied by the visible provision of benefits to the majority.

In fact, according to the OECD (2004d), European governments generally spend 20–30 per cent of GDP on welfare payments. In other words at least half of all government expenditure is not on the provision of public goods (despite the assumption of the studies that challenge tax competition) but on transfers between citizens. Even if the government manages these transfers without any cost (which it cannot), it is impossible for MB > MC as they are purely redistributional rather than productive; there is no output of public goods.

Public choice

Recent studies in tax competition have tried to take account of this, some of them drawing on public choice theory. Effectively a way of analysing government action by subjecting it to the same processes as we would the actions of private persons, this is one of the more powerful bodies of literature available to counter the assumption of perfectly omniscient and benevolent governments. It recognises that governments are composed of and operated not by machines but by individuals, whose livelihoods and influence are generally dependent on the increase in government power and activity; governments are therefore run by people who have a vested interest in the increase of government revenues.

Public choice theory began with Brennan and Buchanan in the 1970s, but its absorption into the study of tax competition gained ground only in the late 1990s (see Edwards and Keen, 1996) and is still in its infancy. There are objections from the traditional economists, partly on political grounds from the left (for whom the benefits of public spending are a doctrinal assumption), and partly because it is as yet unquantifiable and therefore unsuited to a mathematical approach.

Public choice theory is, however, a valuable tool in assessing the effects of tax competition. If governments act partly for their own welfare, then we can no longer assume that increased taxation translates directly into increased public welfare. This means that the basis of most of the tax competition studies is false; in the absence of tax competition the level of public expenditure will not be optimal, it will be too high (and the levels of public benefit may still be too low). Therefore if tax competition reduces the levels of government expenditure, it will move them (at least initially) towards rather than away from the optimum.

Opposition to public choice theory rests on the assumption that it is impossible in an electoral system for governments to be self-serving, as voters will act as a check on any such tendencies. This is naive, however; democracy may theoretically exert some control over government, but in practice its effect is severely constrained. First, modern democracies tend to be oligarchic, offering a fairly limited range of choice on major issues. Second, modern governments are more than the politicians elected to govern them, and tend to have their own bureaucratic growth that politicians can rarely tackle in more than a few isolated areas (and will not do so without strong incentives, such as those provided by tax competition). Third, of course, democracy is a very inefficient check on government power; in the absence of a strong (and strongly defended) constitution there is no check on a majority, and there is a great temptation for politicians to use redistributive taxation to build a coalition of support funded by the minority.

Once government expenditure is subjected to public choice analysis, the benefits of tax competition become apparent. Tax competition acts as a restraint on individual governments' ability to raise taxes; politicians still face demands from their electorates for improved public services, but if this cannot be done through increased taxation they are forced to make the public sector more efficient and better directed. Tax competition therefore increases public welfare, by reducing waste and inefficiencies and allowing more public goods to be provided at a lower cost. Indeed, international tax competition is essential because, unlike in other sectors of the economy, there are few other effective constraints on government inefficiencies.

4 THE EFFECTS OF TAX COMPETITION

We have already seen that many economic studies of tax competition predict a dangerous 'race to the bottom', with tax rates being progressively reduced to zero. Many politicians share this fear; in June 2000 Dutch Finance Minister Bos, in a speech to the OECD, warned of 'not just a "race to the bottom" but a "race to public poverty" … where total tax income of the countries becomes too low for governments to finance a sustainable and sufficient level of public services'. But is this justified, or merely panic?

Although tax competition is credited (particularly by the OECD) with bringing about much-needed reductions in tax rates (particularly on capital) in the 1980s, it is worth pointing out that some of the heat in the arguments against tax competition is not justified by its observable effects.

Analysis of tax rates in Europe does not suggest an imminent race to the bottom; tax revenues as a percentage of GDP across the European Union remained almost static from 1995 to 2002, fluctuating slightly but ending the period almost where they began. Indeed, over the period most EU national governments managed to increase their tax revenues as a percentage of GDP; the only ones that saw substantial reductions were those countries that deliberately chose to reduce tax as a matter of policy to stimulate their economies (Ireland, Estonia, the Slovak Republic and Latvia).

Table 4 **Average EU tax as a percentage of GDP**

1995	46.1
1996	46.7
1997	46.8
1998	46.5
1999	47.0
2000	46.4
2001	45.9
2002	45.3
2003	45.8

Source: EU (Eurostat) (2004)

Even if we consider a longer timescale, the view that emerges is not a decimation of tax revenues caused by tax competition, but merely a slowing of the increase in tax rates from the high levels of the 1970s.

The alternative argument against tax competition is that it shifts tax burdens from mobile capital to labour; the theoretical problems with this contention are examined in Chapter 7, but even if theoretically valid it does not appear to be true in practice: the balance of the burden has remained remarkably constant. Indeed, if anything there has been a slight shift away from the taxation of labour towards taxing capital – precisely the opposite of the predictions from the opponents of tax competition. Indeed France, one of the main opponents of tax competition, managed to increase the weighting towards taxing capital over the period (up from 19 per cent of total tax revenues to 21.1 per cent).

A likely explanation of these figures is that the theory that reducing taxes on capital increases wealth is true, and that we are seeing the Laffer curve in action. The reductions in the headline rates of tax in the 1980s therefore led to increased investment and

Table 5 **Percentage of tax from capital, labour and consumption**

Year	Capital	Labour	Consumption
1995	19.0	52.7	28.2
1996	20.1	52.2	27.8
1997	20.9	51.3	27.8
1998	21.0	51.0	28.0
1999	21.4	50.3	28.3
2000	22.0	50.0	28.0
2001	21.3	50.7	28.0
2002	20.6	50.9	28.6

Source: EU (European Commission) (2004b: 274–5)

increased income from capital, so the actual tax take from capital increased as the rates fell.

In addition we probably have strong tax competition preventing governments from putting into practice an unspoken desire to increase the taxation of capital, but if so then let us be thankful that tax competition does exist. It seems far more likely that this is a demonstration of the role of tax competition as one of a range of different forces pushing politicians in different directions, and that a dynamic equilibrium has, at least for now, been reached.

A study by the European Parliament (Patterson and Serrano, 1998) agrees with this assumption: 'Tax competition has not had the effect of *reducing* tax bases, either within the EU or the OECD. However, the increase in overall taxation over the last ten years has only been marginal compared to that in the previous ten or twenty.' As to the tax mix, there have been reductions in corporate tax rates (although in many countries, such as the UK, this has been accompanied by a widening of the corporate tax base so that the effective rates have actually increased), but overall 'over the period 1985–94 there was a shift from taxes on labour to taxes on other production factors'.

The tax competition debate therefore needs to be approached with caution. The predictions of a total collapse of government revenues, at least from mobile tax bases, have simply not come true. Tax competition, however, clearly appears to exist. In fact, because the main effect of tax competition is to act as a restraint on governments' ability to raise taxes, so long as governments believe that it works (which they clearly do, since they are making such efforts to stamp it out) then it will. There must therefore be countervailing pressures to increase taxes that are being mainly neutralised by tax competition.

What the opponents of tax competition are really arguing therefore is that taxes, particularly on capital, are currently too low and should be increased. This makes it even more likely that tax competition is actually a beneficial force, preventing damaging increases in tax levels on savings and investment.

5 TOWARDS A NEW APPROACH TO TAX COMPETITION

A new theoretical approach to tax competition is needed. This must be rooted in the real world, and be flexible enough to analyse the impact of tax competition without simplifying the world to the point where the unrealistic nature of its assumptions invalidate its findings. Unfortunately this means that it is difficult to quantify the impact of competition, but that does not invalidate its conclusions.

First, tax competition clearly reduces levels of taxation, and therefore (in the long term) levels of government expenditure. This does not in practice, however, appear to be a substantial shift, except in a few small countries that choose to actively engage in aggressive tax competition in order to attract relatively substantial amounts of foreign capital in relation to their size. Although there are tax havens with effective tax rates of zero, most established industrialised countries have managed to maintain substantial (and historically high) levels of tax on capital and other mobile tax bases.

Tax competition is therefore clearly not the only factor driving the choice of tax rates. It seems likely that it acts as a counterweight to various pressures for increased government expenditure, whether from groups within the electorate, a momentum for increased spending driven by natural inefficiencies, or internal pressures from within the bureaucracy. Public choice theory is one useful way to explain these tendencies, but is not a necessary one.

Tax competition is only necessarily harmful if it reduces levels of government expenditure from an efficient optimum. This is only a valid assumption if tax levels, and benefits from public goods, would naturally be at their optimum levels in the absence of tax competition. The various factors outlined below suggest that, in the real rather than the theoretical world, this optimum is unlikely to be reached.

The impact of taxation on wealth generation appears to be imperfectly understood by governments and their electorates. This means that tax levels are likely to be too high, because even if potential public expenditure is assessed by comparing marginal benefits with marginal costs, the marginal costs used are liable to be too low if the knock-on effect of taxation on wealth generation (whether savings levels, labour or other factors) is not given sufficient weight by the government and electorate. In addition, the higher cost of public sector procurement means that the benefits from public spending are lower than might be expected.

Global capital market efficiency is also increased by the use of tax havens. In theory improved cooperation between national governments (in terms of the tax systems of high-tax countries, rather than global rate harmonisation) could make this unnecessary, and the OECD and the EU are doing valuable work along these lines, but in reality progress is slow and in the meantime the use of tax havens is invaluable in increasing global capital efficiency and therefore global wealth.

Expenditure choice would also need to be purely attuned to the needs of the population, if governments are to be efficient without tax competition. In reality, there is a tendency for governments to create electoral coalitions in which those who suffer the highest marginal rates of tax (whether on capital or labour) are likely to be electorally insignificant. Tax competition creates a counter-weight to this tendency, at the worst allowing such minorities an 'exit' strategy but at best ensuring that their needs are given a fair weighting.

There are therefore clear inefficiencies, practical, theoretical and allocational, in public spending in the absence of tax competi-tion, which the presence of tax competition can reduce. By acting as a constraint on tax levels, tax competition should prompt governments to spend funds more efficiently for maximum public benefits and so, at least initially, force a move towards greater efficiency, with the only risk being that it will go too far and will reduce tax levels below their optimal point.

Janeba and Schjelderup (2004) combined some of these factors and concluded that tax competition was highly likely to be beneficial. Another recent study (Parry, 2001) tried to quantify the effect of tax competition and suggested that, if governments were otherwise perfectly efficient, tax competition would reduce levels of capital taxation by 3 per cent. To put this in perspective, levels of capital taxation in the EU are roughly 20 per cent of GDP (EU (European Commission), 2004b), so a reduction of 3 per cent of expected capital taxation receipts amounts to a reduction in government revenue of roughly 0.5 per cent of GDP. In other words, even if governments are perfectly efficient, the damage caused by tax competition will amount to government spending being 0.5 per cent of GDP below the optimum. Of course, this is on the assumption that governments are perfectly efficient, and so perfectly benevolent and knowledgeable; if government inefficien-cies lead to taxes being more than 0.5 per cent of GDP above their optimum then tax competition is likely to be beneficial.

6 TAX COMPETITION IN PRACTICE – THE USE OF TAX HAVENS

This study has so far concentrated on the theory of tax competition. As we have seen, this leads to oversimplification and therefore gives answers that are unlikely to be relevant to the real world. It is essential therefore to examine briefly the ways in which tax competition operates in practice, in order to assess more reliably its likely impact.

Introduction

Tax competition is based on the theory that people respond to tax differentials by moving tax bases (such as investment capital, production or labour) to jurisdictions where tax rates are lowest. Jurisdictions with very low rates of tax, known as 'tax havens',[1] are clearly the places where this competition will be most fierce, and so tax competition between high-tax countries (such as most of western Europe) and tax havens would be expected to show the greatest practical results.

The mere existence of low-tax jurisdictions, however, is not enough to bring about effective tax competition; it must also be possible for them to be used effectively. This can be difficult: before the removal of exchange controls in the 1980s the use of tax

---

1   '*Paradis fiscale*' in French, but this is a mistranslation: they are not heavens but havens, safe harbours for your money.

havens was often very problematic, as money could not easily be moved to them. In recent years this problem has been removed, and (as shown above) international capital movements have grown enormously, but there are still barriers to the use of tax havens. These barriers now mainly take the form of anti-avoidance (or 'anti-haven') legislation within the tax laws of the high-tax countries.

All countries have different tax laws, but the co-development of tax systems within the global market has made it possible to lay down some general principles that are reflected in most circumstances. This is partly due to countries copying what seems to work elsewhere, and partly through the valuable work of the OECD in trying to reduce tax disincentives to international trade and investment caused by incongruities between national tax systems.

Since tax competition is often discussed in a vacuum, as a purely theoretical issue, this means that the findings of such studies are often of little practical use. In order to properly examine tax competition in the real world, and the moves being made to restrict it, it is necessary to have some understanding of the way in which it is used in practice. In fact tax competition is less strong than some of its opponents suggest, largely because it is made less efficient by the significant barriers that already exist to taxpayers' ability to take advantage of tax havens.

The basics of international taxation

There are two main bases on which states claim the right to levy tax: the *source* principle (under which governments tax income that arises in their jurisdiction) and the *residence* principle (under

which they tax all income belonging to people living in their jurisdiction, no matter from where it arises). Some countries adopt a
territorial tax system, under which they use only the source principle and do not tax foreign income of their residents; others
adopt a residence-only basis, in which local-source income of
non-residents is tax exempt. In practice, however, most countries
use both the source and residence systems so that foreign income
tends to be taxed twice, once where it is earned and once where
the owner lives.[2]

As an example, if a UK national, living in the UK, deposits
money in a Canadian bank and earns interest on it, that interest
will be taxed by Canada under the source principle and by the UK
under the residence principle.

This would make most cross-border investment unprofitable
if both countries levied tax at their full rates. Therefore in practice
these charges are generally mitigated by rules to avoid this 'double
taxation'. There are two main ways of doing this: the exemption
method (under which the home country gives up its right to tax
overseas income) and the credit method (where the home country
reduces its tax demands by the amount already paid to the source
country).

To continue our example, if the UK government operated the
exemption method it would not tax its citizen's interest from the
Canadian bank. In fact the UK operates the credit method, under
which it taxes the interest but then gives credit for the Canadian

2   The UK is somewhat complex. In general it uses both the source and residence
     principles, but in some areas it adopts a territorial system where it does not tax
     residents on their foreign income (such as the 'non-domicile' rule, discussed fur-
     ther below) and in other areas it uses a residence-only basis and does not tax non-
     residents on UK-source income (such as the Eurobond exemptions discussed in
     the chapter on the EU Savings Tax Directive).

tax already paid (i.e. the UK tax would be reduced by the amount of Canadian tax paid). The investor would therefore pay 25 per cent tax in Canada (in fact a withholding tax deducted by the Canadian bank) and a further 15 per cent in the UK (assuming he is a higher-rate taxpayer), giving a total tax liability equal to the full UK rate of 40 per cent. This ensures that international activity is taxed in the same way as purely domestic business.

This is frequently further modified by the use of double tax treaties, bilateral agreements between governments that effectively share out their taxing rights. In this example the tax treaty between Canada and the UK restricts the Canadian tax to 10 per cent, so that the UK national pays 10 per cent Canadian tax and a further 30 per cent in the UK (note that the taxpayer still pays the same total amount; it has just been divided differently between the two governments). In this way the countries ensure that the decision as to where to invest is tax neutral (because the UK resident pays the same overall amount of tax wherever he invests) and the two countries agree to share the overall tax. The OECD has done much useful work in the promotion of double tax treaties in order to reduce the tax distortions in international capital markets, and many of the double tax treaties in force are based on its model.

The use of tax havens by individuals

The most dramatic use of tax havens by individuals is to become resident in such a haven. If your country of residence has only very low or zero taxes, the only tax paid would be on the source principle (and it is generally easy to ensure that investments are chosen that do not give rise to source-based taxes). Tax haven residence, however, is often difficult or undesirable on other grounds, as tax residence usually requires spending more than half the year physically present in the country and tax havens that do not impose taxes on their residents tend to be remote or expensive to live in.

In addition, it is not enough to become resident in the tax haven: one also has to stop being tax resident in any high-tax country. Many countries make it more difficult to lose your tax residence status than it is to acquire it: the UK, for example, continues to tax its nationals as if they were still tax resident if they have left for only 'occasional residence abroad' (Income & Corporation Taxes Act 1988, s334), and the USA taxes all its citizens on their worldwide income, whether or not they are actually resident there. This can lead to 'dual residence', where one is treated as tax resident (and therefore taxed on your worldwide income) in more than one country because each uses different rules for determining residence. Obviously being simultaneously tax resident in two high-tax countries would be disastrous; this is usually avoided by double tax treaties (under which one country will give up its taxing rights), but most countries do not enter into double tax treaties with tax havens and so dual residence is used by the high-tax countries to continue to tax the worldwide income of people with tax haven residence.

Benefiting from tax havens by becoming resident in one therefore carries high costs (both economic and personal), as it generally prevents all but rare visits to other countries. This use of tax havens, although it appeals to the popular imagination, is therefore relatively rare (although for some of the seriously rich, such as Monaco-based retailer Philip Green, it is still worthwhile). Some individuals manage to be permanently non-resident in any country, but this involves almost continuous travel (although there is now a permanently touring liner, ResidenSea, on which tax exiles can buy an apartment to assist with this), and so it is generally unpopular.

The more common use of tax havens for individuals is therefore as a source of income rather than a location for residence. Income that arises in a tax haven (such as interest from a haven bank account or dividends from a haven collective investment scheme) will suffer little or no tax in the haven (i.e. low source-basis tax). There is of course still the individual's country of residence which will tax this income (and all his worldwide income) on the residence basis, which would negate the advantages of the tax haven. This may be avoided, however, in one of two ways. Although the country of residence may theoretically impose taxes on foreign income, it can only do so practically if its tax authorities have knowledge of that income. It is therefore common for tax havens to have strong privacy laws that protect investors' personal information from enquirers (including foreign tax authorities). The best-known of these was Switzerland, which introduced banking secrecy to protect Jewish customers from Nazi confiscation, and there remains a genuine strong feeling in many of these countries that privacy is about more than just tax avoidance. Concealment of taxable sources from one's home country tax authorities is risky, as discovery often carries the risk of fines (and in some cases potential prosecution for criminal tax evasion). Many investors therefore prefer to seek a legal route to avoid tax.

The legal avoidance of tax is often possible, as countries give incentives for particular types of people or for particular investments. Some countries simply do not tax overseas income (Panama was the best known for tax planning, but France also exempts many forms of foreign income). Many countries tax capital gains at lower rates than they do income: it may then be possible to use tax havens to convert income into capital (for example, instead of investing money in shares, where the dividends will be taxed as they are received, it is possible to invest in a tax haven investment fund; the fund then invests the capital in shares and receives its dividends tax free; the investor then sells his stake in the fund, with its investments and tax-free growth, giving himself a capital gain). Again this is a perfectly legal use of tax havens.

One of the greatest exemptions for overseas income is given by the UK. Individuals who are not domiciled in the UK (in loose terms non-UK nationals) are exempt from tax on their non-UK income, provided they do not bring it into the country. This is a deliberate move by the UK government to attract wealthy foreigners to live here: the UK benefits from their presence (particularly their spending and employment, plus other investment in the case of senior executives of foreign businesses), and indeed the current Labour government has reviewed this exemption and appears to have decided to keep it.

The UK's non-domicile rule appears to be remarkably successful in attracting wealthy foreigners. Reports in 2003 suggested that half of those earning over £100,000 p.a. in the UK were non-UK nationals. At the top end of the spectrum, analysis of the 2004 *Sunday Times* Rich List for the UK suggests that 28 of the 100 richest individuals in the UK, controlling 43 per cent of the wealth of the top 100, appear likely to be non-UK-domiciled. Among the super-rich this tendency is even more marked. Of the top fifteen in the Rich List, eleven (starting with Russian oil oligarch Roman Abramovich, the richest man in the UK) appear likely to be benefiting from the non-domicile exemption. Together these eleven control an estimated £33 billion of assets. Clearly it is difficult to judge the extent to which the non-domicile rule is essential to attracting these wealthy residents: the UK presumably also has other attractions, but it seems unlikely that they would be enough to outweigh a 40 per cent tax charge. The UK government also clearly believes that the exemption is valuable, as it has survived much political opposition and a number of reviews.

Tax advice is a global profession, and tax havens provide specific products to enable taxpayers to take advantage of the exemptions in their country's tax laws. This leads to a symbiotic relationship between certain high-tax countries and associated tax havens, and so the bulk of the Channel Islands offshore personal banking sector is designed for these individuals who are resident in the UK but benefit from the non-domicile rule.

It is therefore possible for individuals to use tax havens perfectly legally to reduce their tax liability without having to emigrate, but these uses depend on the precise tax system of the home country and require careful and ongoing planning.

The use of tax havens by companies

Like individuals, companies are generally taxed on both the source and residence principles. This means that it is not usually worthwhile setting up a company in a tax haven to run a UK-based business; as a UK source of income, the business profits would be taxed in the UK anyway.

Instead the most common use of tax havens by companies is to set up a subsidiary in a haven that supplies services to other group companies. Generally these are either group finance companies (lending money to other companies in the group that need funds for capital projects), group insurance companies (which insure members of the group but do not act as general insurers for outside clients) and group IP (intellectual property) companies (which hold the group's intellectual property such as patents, trademarks or copyrights). These tax haven companies then charge the other group companies for their services, and receive interest, insurance premiums, royalties or other payments from members of the group. The group's overall pre-tax profits are not affected by this activity because the money all stays within the group (apart from the relatively minor costs of setting up and running these companies), but profits are diverted from companies in high-tax countries to those in tax havens, reducing the group's total tax costs.

The types of activity (such as finance, insurance and IP) are chosen because they are highly mobile and therefore can be relocated to tax havens at a low cost. There is generally little point in setting up a manufacturing plant in the Caribbean, as the cost of shipping raw materials in and finished products out would cancel out any tax advantage. In recent years, however, there has been an increase in more accessible jurisdictions offering low effective tax rates for less mobile operations, either explicitly (for example, Ireland, with its 12 per cent corporate tax rate, and Estonia, which does not tax companies on their profits) or in a disguised way by offering tax incentives for particular types of activity (see below for more details). This has widened the range of suitable activities whereby companies can take advantage of tax competition, and has therefore made tax competition more effective.

Tax authority action against corporate use of tax havens

As we saw with individuals, it is not as easy as many imagine to take advantage of tax havens. For companies, tax authorities often have a wide range of 'anti-avoidance' laws to reduce the opportunities for companies to take advantage of tax competition. These rules generally make tax competition less effective, as they either reduce the number of companies that can take advantage of it, or reduce the proportion of their profits that can be protected in this way, or simply increase the incidental costs of using tax havens.

Residence

First, the tax haven company must be properly resident in the tax haven. Like an individual, if a company is resident in a high-tax jurisdiction then it will be subject to tax there on its worldwide profits. This involves more than simply legally incorporating a subsidiary in a tax haven; it must genuinely be run from there.

The usual stipulation is that a company should be resident in the country where it is 'managed and controlled', which means that board-level decisions about the subsidiary must be taken in a tax haven. Tax authorities are becoming experienced at challenging companies that they believe are run from their country; one of the UK Inland Revenue's early successes was in 1906 when it successfully taxed the South African-based De Beers on the basis that its board meetings were held in London, and again in 1959 it proved that a Kenyan company's board meetings, held in Kenya, were a sham and in fact the company was run from the UK.

Controlled Foreign Company (CFC) legislation

The tax authorities still have some successes with the residence rule, but tax planners soon taught their clients how to ensure that a tax haven subsidiary is genuinely run from the haven so that it merely added to the cost of using it: reducing rather than negating the benefits of tax competition. This would make tax competition less efficient, and therefore less effective, but for large multinational groups the costs would not be significant.

More dangerous is the anti-avoidance legislation generally known as CFC (Controlled Foreign Company) rules (the US equivalent is less memorably known as 'sub-part F'). Under these rules, tax authorities suspend the usual principles of international tax and give themselves the power to tax companies on the profits of their tax haven subsidiaries. A UK company that owned a subsidiary group finance company in the Cayman Islands, for example, might therefore have to pay UK tax on the profits of that Cayman subsidiary as they arose, rather than waiting until they were paid as dividends. Clearly this would negate the tax advantages of the haven.

If CFC legislation were sufficiently tight, it would make the use of tax havens by companies almost impossible (except by disguising the control of the subsidiary, which would be practically difficult and also counter-productive, as its profits could then not be included in the group's accounts). Fortunately most countries leave broad exemptions in their CFC legislation. For example, the UK rules do not apply provided that tax avoidance is not 'one of the main reasons for the company's existence' (Income & Corporation Taxes Act 1988, s748(3)). Fortunately tax havens tend to offer numerous other non-tax advantages; for example, in the financial services sector they generally have much less burdensome regulation than EU countries.

Transfer pricing

If profits can be diverted to a tax-exempt group company based in a tax haven, by group companies in high-tax countries paying it for services, then even more tax could be saved (without reducing overall group pre-tax profits) if the tax haven company 'over-charged' the other group companies for its services. This would raise the profits of the tax haven company and lower the profits of the related companies in higher tax jurisdictions. Most countries have introduced 'transfer pricing' rules to prevent this, effectively saying that payments to associated companies will not be deductible expenses for tax purposes unless they are a fair market price for the services actually received.

These rules prevent the excessive loss of taxable profits from high-tax jurisdictions; effectively they ensure that tax competition is fair because the tax follows the underlying activity. If the tax base is not genuinely moved to a low-tax jurisdiction, then tax will not be reduced.

The economic effect of tax haven use

Multinational corporate groups therefore commonly use tax havens to divert profits from high-tax to low-tax jurisdictions, by setting up subsidiary companies that provide services to other group companies in return for a fee.

The effect of this is not, however, to allow shareholders to reap tax-free profits. The tax-free profits are earned by the group's tax haven company, but that is only a subsidiary of the group; in order to pay its profits out to shareholders they must first be paid as a dividend to the group's parent company, at which point they will be taxed (the parent company is generally situated in a high-tax country, because it is far too difficult to manage the group's whole business from a tax haven).

This means that in order to remain tax free these profits are effectively trapped in the tax haven subsidiary. The only way in which they can be used is for the subsidiary to lend them back out to the other group companies. This produces a virtuous circle, as those group companies then pay interest on these loans, transferring more profits to the tax haven subsidiary. It also means that tax haven profits of a multinational group are generally used to reinvest in the group, by funding expansion projects. These tax haven companies are therefore often referred to as 'piggy banks', safe deposits for group capital. As many governments (including, notably, the current Labour government, as shown by Gordon Brown's change to the tax treatment of dividends for UK pension funds) are generally keen to promote reinvestment within corporations rather than dividends, one might have expected such governments to support this use of tax havens.[3]

This is in fact an example of how tax havens promote investment and the growth of wealth, and help to avoid some of the unintended consequences of tax systems. Tax can still be collected when the company's profits flow out to the shareholders (either when dividends are paid or when the shareholders sell the shares for a profit), but it seems perverse for governments to encourage corporate reinvestment and yet tax the profits that are needed to fund it. By sensible use of tax haven subsidiaries companies can avoid this problem and create an internal pool of capital to fund investment and expansion.

---

3   That is not to say that such reinvestment within companies rather than the dispersal of profits for reinvestment by shareholders is generally a good thing – merely that many governments support it.

Onshore tax havens

The activity discussed so far concerns traditional tax havens, generally small countries (commonly remote islands, leading to the common description of tax havens as being 'offshore'), and the action taken against them by large industrialised countries. There is more to tax competition than this, however. Many high-tax countries also engage in tax competition, by having aspects of their tax systems that amount to tax haven activity.

Within Europe, Ireland has acted as a corporate tax haven for a number of years: despite having a general corporation tax rate of 30 per cent it introduced special 10 per cent tax rates for companies engaging in particular activities in specific geographic locations (including financial services in the depressed Dublin dockyards and international distribution services around the rural Shannon airport). These are now being dismantled, having been declared illegal by the EU under its 'State Aid' rules (see Chapter 11), but, as a replacement, Ireland is adopting a general 12 per cent tax rate for all companies. The specific 10 per cent rates were very successful, attracting substantial activity and helping to fuel a boom in Ireland's economy (also partly driven by substantial transfers in from EU funds). It is now thought that Ireland is well placed (geographically close to major markets, an EU member so able to benefit from free movement of goods throughout the EU, and with a well-educated workforce able to expand without damaging wage inflation as the diaspora returns) to attract foreign capital with its new relatively low tax rates.

A new EU entrant that is looking to benefit from tax competition is Estonia, with no tax on company profits. Estonia has celebrated its escape from communism by embracing the free market, and offers a low-tax economy with all the trading benefits of EU membership, and now through its tax reforms it is looking to attract manufacturing industry, to boost its economy and increase employment opportunities for its citizens.

The non-domicile rules have been examined already, but other UK tax haven attributes are designed to help the City of London, and bring in substantial wealth in the form of financial trading (providing high salaries, office rent and support jobs) and associated legal and accounting work. The best known of these is probably the Eurobond exemption (discussed in more detail in Chapter 8), which allows multinational companies to raise finance through London without their investors suffering UK tax on their income. There is also a special treatment for investment fund managers: generally collective investment funds managed in a country would be subject to tax in that country (which is why many of them are based in tax havens), but the UK gives valuable exemptions from this rule in order to help the City of London attract work.

Other European countries offer their own specific tax exemptions. Common ones include special tax exemptions for holding companies or for group management companies for multinationals (the Netherlands was one of the first, but Belgium, Denmark and Spain have followed suit). The advantage of these schemes to the countries offering them is that they tend also to bring highly paid senior executives to live (and spend their money) in the country concerned.

These 'onshore' tax haven activities are not confined to Europe. The USA has a long-standing exemption from tax on bank interest for non-residents, which allows its banks to operate as if they were in a tax haven. It also has some interesting company law provisions (originating in Delaware but now more general thanks to the 'check-the-box' provisions) that allow multinational groups to set up companies in the USA that are 'tax transparent' for US tax purposes (effectively they are treated as partnerships, and therefore, provided the shareholders are not US resident, they are not taxed in the USA on non-US income).

These 'onshore tax havens', tax exemptions in otherwise high-tax countries, have various advantages for tax planners. They are often more accessible, and larger economies can be cheaper to use than traditional tax havens. But most importantly, they are not obvious tax havens. This means that these activities are less likely to attract attention from the home country tax authorities, unlike traditional tax havens, which automatically raise suspicion. In addition, as these 'onshore havens' are otherwise high-tax countries they are likely to have double tax treaties with the home country, which may allow tax-free profits to flow back home too.

These tax exemptions given by otherwise high-tax countries will be discussed further below, but they are arguably damaging in ways that the traditional small island tax havens are not. Not only are they hidden, but in many cases the exemptions are targeted at particular types of industry in a way that distorts investment and so makes the economy less, rather than more, efficient. When governments of high-tax countries, particularly those in Europe, attack traditional tax havens for engaging in 'harmful tax competition', it is useful to remember the tax competition provided by these countries' own distortionary tax exemptions. It is also worth mentioning that tax exemptions for particular types of investment act like subsidies. In general, such implicit subsidies impose the greatest costs on the country providing the subsidies (or tax exemptions) because they distort economic activity and support activities that would otherwise be uneconomic. Therefore the notions of 'competition' and a 'race to the bottom' simply do not apply to these forms of special tax treatment.

7 POLITICAL OPPOSITION TO TAX COMPETITION

Introduction

Despite the benefits there is opposition to tax competition, primarily from three groups: those opposed generally to the benefits of global free markets; governments, which object to restraints on their ability to raise taxes; and certain economists and academics who believe that tax competition leads to sub-optimal levels of government spending.

The first group has already been discussed, and will not be examined in any further detail. A justification *ab initio* of free markets would be disproportionate in this book; such justifications exist already, and we are unlikely to convince the true unbeliever by dealing with the issues here. The third group was dealt with in Chapter 3, and was found to base its objection on unsustainable assumptions that are invalid in the real world.

More worrying is the stance of those governments that generally support global free markets, but draw the line at tax competition. Rather like some large businesses that generally support and benefit from free markets, but which would prefer to have at least a quasi-monopoly position in their own sector, such governments want to enjoy the benefits of global free markets (in terms of rising prosperity for their citizens) while protecting their own powers and privileges.

Many European governments believe that they are losing unacceptable amounts of tax revenue owing to competition from tax havens, and so they find it easiest to form a cartel. One of the main attempts to form a cartel is through the Organisation for Economic Cooperation and Development (OECD). This will be examined in more detail in subsequent chapters, but it is interesting here because it makes some attempt to justify its actions.

The OECD is committed to global free markets, and was founded to foster them, and it accepts that tax competition has been beneficial in reducing taxes from the excessive levels of the 1970s. To justify an attack on what it admits to be a beneficial process, the OECD therefore attempts in its reports to distinguish between 'acceptable' and 'harmful' tax competition. The OECD's 1998 report on tax competition itself is of little help in this, as it assumes that all tax competition is harmful unless it fails, making 'harmful' for the OECD in this regard practically synonymous with 'successful'; the primary indicator of harm in a tax system is that it: 'shift[s] activity from one country to the country providing the preferential tax regime' (OECD, 1998: para 81).

In other words non-harmful tax competition is presumably any tax competition that is not actually very competitive. The OECD reports then give, however, three factors as justifications for classifying some tax competition as harmful:

1 'practices designed to encourage non-compliance with the tax laws of other countries';
2 'practices [that] undermine the ability of each country to decide for itself the allocation of tax burden among mobile and less mobile tax bases'; and

3   'practices [that] distort financial and, indirectly, real
    investment flows'.

We will examine these issues in this chapter.

Harmful because it encourages non-compliance?

This is attacking a classic use of a tax haven, as explained in the previous chapter, in which a person resident in (or otherwise subject to the taxation system of) a highly taxed country places his capital in a tax haven where it can earn untaxed income. While there are many cases where the home country does not tax foreign source income (such as the UK's non-domicile exemption discussed above), most Western countries have a worldwide taxation system that seeks to tax the worldwide income of its residents (or all of its citizens in the case of the USA). This tax haven income therefore does not cease (legally) to become liable to tax merely by being earned offshore: it is still liable to tax and the investor has a duty to report it to his home tax authority. In practice, however, if the investor does not report his income, then the home country can have great difficulties in discovering and taxing it, particularly if the haven country has strong banking secrecy laws.

While I am not seeking to condone dishonesty or criminal activity, from an economic perspective this is merely another example of tax competition: indeed, it is often necessary behaviour in order to take advantage of tax havens. Without the willingness of some to engage in this sort of activity, tax competition would be much less effective and therefore reduce the benefits that flow from it for the rest of us.

Opponents claim that, even if tax competition in the sense

of emigration to a tax haven is acceptable, this type of competition is unfair as the taxpayer continues to enjoy the advantages of the highly taxed country without paying for it. There are several counters to this argument, of which some are country specific. In the EU (and in many countries outside the EU) the avoider will still be paying a substantial amount of VAT (or other consumption taxes) whenever he spends his money; and a citizen of the USA is liable to tax even if he never lives in the country and therefore benefits from it only in the loosest way. Perhaps the best response to this moral objection is that presenting wealthy taxpayers with the choice only of leaving the country or being fleeced is hardly a moral action itself.

In the UK the moral objections are even weaker, as he will be putting himself in no better position than a non-domiciled person who chooses to live in the country. As discussed in the previous chapter, the UK has for many years operated a system whereby wealthy foreigners can come to live indefinitely in the UK but without being subject to tax on income received and kept overseas (in contrast becoming tax resident in almost all other countries makes one liable to that country's tax on one's worldwide income). This is not a principled position but a pragmatic one: the UK government deliberately keeps this system in order to attract wealthy foreigners (and their spending) to the UK, which it does very successfully. From an absolute moral standpoint, however, it is difficult to see any difference between a wealthy foreigner considering living in the UK and a wealthy national considering leaving it, and so it is difficult to argue that a UK national is acting immorally by putting himself in the same position as his non-domiciled neighbour.

For companies the position is simpler; they usually cannot

emigrate, and so without this process will be denied some of the benefits of tax competition. Although governments deliberately use their tax systems to attract companies in, they are less willing to let them out. This trap works by an interaction of two rules. First, many tax systems deem a company to be resident in their country (and hence subject to its taxes) if it is incorporated there. This means that a company cannot generally change its tax residence without changing its country of incorporation. Second, it is impossible in many countries for a company to change its country of incorporation: its registration is its very existence, so a company (for example) trying to change its incorporation from the UK to Bermuda will be treated as having been liquidated and as having transferred all its assets to a newly formed Bermudan company (albeit with the same shareholders). This will trigger a taxable capital gain, as if the UK company had sold all its assets at their then market value, with a consequent tax charge. Companies that have no particular reason other than historical accident to be in a country, therefore, and which may have no need to remain there and may indeed have no business or assets there, are trapped into paying its taxes, with no escape but the allegedly improper use of tax havens. In fact, companies rarely rely on concealment in their tax avoidance, and use some of the other devices (such as offshore group finance companies) discussed above in order to take advantage of tax competition.

On an international level there is a further argument against this attack on tax competition: it is effectively demanding that the tax haven countries act as unpaid tax enforcers for the high-tax countries, whether by taxing the high-tax countries' taxpayers directly or reporting their income to the home authorities. There is a long-established principle that countries do not enforce each other's taxes, and it is remarkably high-handed for the OECD states to insist that the tax havens (many of them far from wealthy) act as unpaid tax enforcers for them. Indeed, if an individual acts illegally by not declaring income derived from companies operating from a tax haven, this is no different from any other form of tax evasion (such as that which tends to occur when a builder is paid in cash). It is surely for the government of the country of residence of the individual to enforce its tax laws, in both these cases, not for other countries to do so on behalf of the government of the country of residence. The government should also set tax rates at levels that do not discourage compliance.

Harmful because it prevents allocation of tax burden?

It is easier, runs this argument, for certain types of activity (notably capital investment) than others to move to tax havens. As we saw when looking at the use of tax havens, the most common forms of tax avoidance through tax havens do tend to involve the transfer of capital rather than persons. Tax competition in relation to mobile factors of production will therefore naturally be higher, and taxes on mobile factors of production lower. In order to maintain their expenditure levels, governments will have to increase taxes on the less mobile factors of production, particularly labour, but also, perhaps, land.

First, there is no reason why labour should be excluded from tax competition; not so long ago it was perfectly normal for the British to take jobs across the globe. It may be easier to move capital to a bank in the Caribbean than to take your family there, but that should only make tax competition in respect of labour weaker, not virtually non-existent (as the argument implies).

In fact migration into OECD member countries averaged over 3 million each year in the period 1990–95 (OECD figures), and across the OECD as a whole foreigners averaged 6.25 per cent of the population. Compare this with cross-border investment, which is on average 2.6 per cent of GDP (see Chapter 1), and labour mobility does not seem insignificant.

Second, this objection misses the whole point of tax competition: it is supposed to prompt governments to reduce their expenditure, not simply to seek taxes elsewhere. The objection is particularly invidious, as it implies that governments object to visibly taxing the mass of their electorate (workers, who are also, of course, the recipients of most government spending) when they can tax them indirectly (through taxes on business) or tax the 'rich' (taxes on capital). The argument seems to be that the electorate would not accept the true cost of government programmes if they were visible, in which case, in a democracy, such programmes should not be run.

In an efficient international market, taxes on capital above the value of the public services received by the taxpaying business will force firms to cut costs to maintain the return to their shareholders. This tends to pass the burden of capital taxes on to labour, through reduced wages or increased unemployment. In that case discussion of the allocation of the tax burden between labour and capital is meaningless, but that is not how politicians generally see the world.

Harmful because it distorts?

This is probably the most economic rather than political objection to tax competition. Tax competition, it is claimed, distorts business decisions and causes capital and effort to be allocated based on the tax treatment rather than the underlying return. If this is true then it is a serious problem, as the free market economy is made less efficient if the pricing signals of the market are being disguised by discriminatory taxation.

To investigate this problem it is helpful to recall that there are two types of capital flow, the direction of which is affected by tax competition: portfolio investment (where capital from a number of investors is pooled and invested elsewhere, often without their involvement in the investment decisions) and direct investment (where investors direct their capital into a large percentage stake in a particular enterprise). The best examples of tax haven portfolio investments are the 'retail' collective investment funds marketed from (among many other tax jurisdictions) Jersey, or the investment of deposits by a Cayman Islands bank, and an example of direct foreign investment would be Nissan's car assembly plant near Sunderland in the UK.

A third possibility, the distortion of the international labour market by tax competition, is generally ignored by the OECD governments, as they do not expect any significant number of workers to relocate. As shown above, this is possibly short-sighted, and there is no reason why tax competition should not still be effective in the labour market.

Portfolio investment is unlikely to lead to the distortion of capital flows by tax competition, for the simple reason that it is very rare for capital to be ultimately invested in the country in which it is pooled. The use of tax havens in this regard is to allow the capital of a number of investors, usually from a variety of high-tax countries, to be pooled and collectively invested in business operations, usually themselves in a variety of high-tax countries, without a significant additional layer of tax at the pooling stage. A collective investment scheme located in a high-tax country is likely to be a taxable entity, leading to triple taxation (the business, the collective vehicle and the investor). National rules may mitigate this, but they generally operate effectively only if the three levels are all in the same country, which makes them unsuitable for pools with international investors or investments.

Portfolio investment is therefore not distorted by tax havens (except beneficially as it removes barriers to collective investment), as it affects only the location of the pool, not that of the final investment. As discussed above, this use of tax havens to remove barriers to the efficient working of the global capital market is one of the advantages of tax competition.

Is direct investment subject to harmful distortion by tax competition through the decision as to where to invest being affected by the taxation regimes of the alternative countries being considered? At first glance this is the case, but only on a superficial level. On the assumption that, in a democracy, the government is providing the people only with the services they want at a cost they are willing to pay, then a high level of taxation is simply part of the local culture, just like an unwillingness to work productively after lunch or a propensity to strike. Business taxation in this case is simply another form of pay for the workforce, albeit one paid indirectly and received by them in kind in the form of government services. In this case the efficient functioning of the market is not affected by businesses making location decisions based on the levels of taxation; it is equivalent to it making decisions based on the likely wage demands from the workforce, and a workforce that is too expensive (whether in terms of direct wage demands or indirect demands via taxation) will find itself priced out of the international market.

If the tax revenues are being spent in ways that are beneficial for businesses rather than the population then again it will not be distortionary if businesses consider these taxes in their decision-making; the government will merely be another supplier and the business will decide whether it is sufficiently efficient when compared with other suppliers.

If taxes are being levied to fund projects that are neither desired (and valued) by the people nor beneficial to business, then precisely why (especially in a democracy) are they being levied at all? In this case, if tax competition is responsible for reducing tax revenue so that expenditure that is not wanted (other than by politicians) is not incurred, it can only be beneficial for the people at large.

If we examine the different types of tax haven, they seem to fall into three different groups, being those with:

1 no (or virtually no) taxes at all;
2 tax exemptions for foreign investors or foreign operations; and
3 specific tax exemptions for particular industries.

The first is extremely rare, and the second is what is today thought of as being the classic tax haven. States falling into either of these categories are almost exclusively small and relatively inaccessible, and therefore attract only portfolio (rather than direct) investment in any significant quantities. As we have seen above, it is only direct investment (and arguably not even that) in respect of which tax competition can lead to distortions of investment decisions, and so these types of tax haven are not an economic problem.

It is therefore only the third type of tax haven that could be likely to lead to distortions in economic decision-making. The danger is that these exemptions can distort not only the location of investment (which is probably not a market distortion anyway; see above) but also the sector into which the investment flows (if nothing else, these sectors will be able to make a higher after-tax return and so will attract increased investment). This is a potentially serious problem, and one that the OECD is right to address, though, as has been mentioned above, it is arguable that the country providing the tax incentives suffers to the greatest degree.

But in any case, which rogue states fall into this third category, the harmful tax regimes? As discussed in the previous chapter, primarily they are the USA, the UK and the other countries of the OECD. It is therefore the specific, industry-targeted tax exemptions operated by these countries, and these alone, which cause economic distortions and weaken the efficiency of the free market.

8 ATTACKS ON TAX COMPETITION I –
THE EU SAVINGS TAX DIRECTIVE

A number of different bodies are using various approaches to attempt to reduce tax competition, either by attacking tax havens directly or by seeking to neutralise their supposed effects. There is a common factor in all the initiatives, however: the close involvement of the major EU governments.

Within the EU, direct taxes (income and corporation taxes, but not VAT) are supposedly under the control of the national governments. As the single market opened up borders within the EU, however, with its guaranteed free movement for people, goods and capital, there have been concerns from the governments of high-tax countries that they will be harmed by tax competition. There have been calls for a full harmonisation of taxes across the EU, including recently by French finance minister Nicolas Sarkozy in September 2004, but so far the Commission has adopted an incremental approach under which it seeks to move towards harmonisation in specific areas only.

Introduction to the directive

Although frequently pronounced dead, the European Union's 'Savings Tax Directive' was finally passed on 24 June 2005, and came into force on 1 July 2005.

This is the widely reported process by which the higher-tax

governments of Europe are hoping to stop their citizens sheltering their savings in low-tax countries. All affected countries now have to either levy a withholding tax on all interest payments to EU residents (most of which must be paid over to the EU government where the recipient is resident) or automatically report the amount of interest paid to the recipient's national tax authority so that they can tax it themselves under the residence principle.

Forcing tax havens to tax interest payments to EU residents is the simplest way of removing tax competition. The rates demanded are 15 per cent for the first three years of operation of the system, 20 per cent (the international norm for tax deductions from bank interest) for the next three years, but a clearly punitive 35 per cent thereafter. Tax will be deducted from interest payments by the payer (whether a bank or other entity), and three-quarters of the tax must be paid to the investor's home government.

Although a 35 per cent withholding tax would remove the incentive for most offshore investment, and hence cripple tax competition, the EU regards it as merely a temporary measure. Indeed, it was introduced as an option only as a way around the tradition in several countries of protecting investors through client confidentiality and banking secrecy. The final aim is clearly automatic reporting, to enable the investor's home authority to impose the full rates of domestic tax and hence neutralise the effect of tax competition, as it ensures that the same tax is paid wherever capital is invested, and the 35 per cent withholding tax is designed merely as an alternative tool.

Opposition to the directive

The European Commission had been pushing for such a scheme

for fifteen years, backed strongly by some of the high-tax governments, but the process was held up for years, primarily by two members of the EU that effectively act as onshore tax havens.

The first, Luxembourg, has for its size a massive financial services sector, fuelled by its tax exemptions for interest payments and strong banking secrecy: it is therefore unwilling to agree to anything that would risk losing any of this business. Indeed, it was the loss of tax revenue to the German government through its citizens putting their money into Luxembourg banks (a process made easier by the removal of border controls in the EU, and by the introduction of the euro) which arguably started this whole process. Austria also has banking secrecy and is involved to a lesser extent in the same sort of financial business as Luxembourg.

The other major EU tax haven, however, is the UK, whose massive $3 trillion eurobond market is tax free. Multinational groups can issue bonds, traded on the London Stock Exchange, and pay interest without any requirement to deduct withholding tax. This allows companies (mainly but not exclusively US and Japanese) to borrow money more cheaply by paying interest to investors gross, and hence again promotes productive investment and so generates employment and wealth. The existence of this market in London brings much wealth to the UK, particularly highly paid financial sector jobs, associated legal and accountancy work and rents and taxes paid by banks and traders.

Both these countries therefore feared that the Savings Tax Directive would damage their national economies: both the Luxembourg bank deposits and the London eurobond market are attractive primarily because they are tax free. It is true that both countries also have reasonably efficient banking and dealing sectors, but no more than many other jurisdictions; if tax had to be imposed because of the EU then there would be no particular reason for this activity to stay in either country.

This relocation risk was one of the strongest arguments used by the UK and Luxembourg. Bank deposits are clearly mobile, and although the eurobond market seems more permanent it has moved once already (from New York: see below) because of tax and would presumably be ready to move again. The Savings Tax Directive would therefore do only harm, not good, since if all savings within the EU were taxed then investors would simply move their money outside. The EU would therefore lose valuable financial sector business and the related income (and employment), but without collecting significantly more tax.

Indeed, there is evidence that capital flight has begun: the Hong Kong Securities & Futures Commission reported that investments in collective investment schemes had soared by 56 per cent in 2003 after years of relatively stable growth. Although the source of these inflowing funds is unknown, there is speculation that it represented European capital moving out before the directive was implemented.

This possibility of capital market mobility is not just a theoretical idea: the London eurobond market was initially formed in 1964 when the USA started levying tax on bond interest, and corporate borrowing (and the associated trading) was swiftly relocated to London. Market mobility is if anything even greater than it was in the 1960s, so the loss of the eurobond markets if a withholding tax were levied would be very rapid.

In the European Union tax measures can be imposed only by unanimous agreement of all member state governments, which means that Luxembourg and the UK could, and did, veto any moves to introduce the savings directive. After several years of strong pressure, however, they extracted valuable concessions and finally gave way. One of the concessions was an exemption from the new rules for existing eurobonds: this was essential as many of them included a clause for automatic redemption if withholding taxes were ever imposed, a factor that proves the importance of the tax exemptions to market location.

Geographical extension of the directive

The agreement between the EU member governments also made the Savings Tax Directive conditional on its rules also being accepted by various non-EU countries, in an attempt to ensure that there was nowhere for these markets to move to. Specifically it must cover:

- the main non-EU European tax havens: Switzerland, Liechtenstein, San Marino, Monaco and Andorra;
- 'dependent or associated territories' of EU members: the Channel Islands, the Isle of Man, the Dutch Antilles and Aruba, and the UK's dependencies in the Caribbean.

The EU has no formal jurisdiction over these countries, but they were clearly chosen because it felt that it could pressure them into agreeing to its demands, owing either to geographic proximity or political or economic ties. The associated territories accepted the EU's demands, generally during 2003/04, after pressure from the UK Treasury that even the UK's Foreign and Commonwealth Office regarded as excessive.

Even so, it was widely thought that the agreement to the Savings Tax Directive by the UK and Luxembourg, and its acceptance by the smaller low-tax jurisdictions, was an irrelevance because the process was conditional on Switzerland also agreeing. The Swiss government was thought to be unlikely to ever agree to anything that might damage its international banking sector.

The Swiss were put under intolerable pressure, however, particularly by Germany (which was losing the most under the old system through its citizens investing in Luxembourg banks) introducing excessive customs checks and administrative inconveniences in an attempt to practically close the Swiss border (the Spanish government has been using similar tactics against Gibraltar). Finally, in June 2004, the Swiss government, after extracting other concessions from the European Union, agreed to sign up to the directive, and in June 2005 the European Union members (in the Council of Ministers) accepted the fifteen bilateral agreements and gave the 'green light' for the directive to come into force, just in time for its due date of 1 July.

Those new member states from eastern Europe, such as Estonia, which have celebrated their escape from communism by repositioning themselves as low-tax dynamic economies may now find their renaissance damaged through having allowed the EU to reverse this policy by imposing Europe-wide taxes.

The effectiveness of the directive

Fortunately the directive is unlikely to destroy tax competition, even from those jurisdictions that have been pressured to implement it.

First it does not, of course, cover all countries: indeed, there need be only one remaining tax haven for tax competition to operate. Tax competition will be seriously weakened, however, especially as many of the major tax havens, and those with the more efficient centres, are covered. Tax competition will survive, but it could take years to regain its current strength.

Second, the directive calls for tax deductions only on investors who are resident in the EU: deposits from the USA and other nations will not be affected, and their citizens will continue to enjoy the benefits of tax competition.

Third, only interest payments are covered, so other forms of tax avoidance will continue to be possible, and tax competition will survive in other areas, particularly business location. Bank deposits and loan capital are clearly the most mobile part of the tax base, however, and therefore the area in which tax competition is most efficient.

Even for EU investors, however, the directive is full of holes and should be easily avoidable; indeed, the Swiss have dubbed it the 'fools' tax' because only those who do not take proper advice will be harmed by it. Without giving tax advice on avoidance methods (which is indeed impossible at this stage), there seem to be two main methods that are likely to be explored in order to avoid the impact of the directive.

First, the bank or other person paying interest is under no obligation to investigate whether or not the person to whom interest is paid is actually the beneficial owner. For example, if a bank in an associated Caribbean territory pays interest to a trustee based in a jurisdiction not subject to the EU's rules, then the bank will not have to deduct tax from that payment unless it is actually informed by the trustee that the beneficiary of the trust is an EU resident. This will help reduce the loss of efficiency in tax competition, as offshore banks will still be able to operate in the jurisdictions where they are most efficient; only the simpler trustee operations will have to move immediately to other territories.

Second, the directive applies only to interest, not to dividends. An EU investor can therefore set up a company in a tax haven, even one subject to the directive, and invest share capital in it. That share capital can then be deposited by the company into a bank in the same territory; as the recipient of the interest earned is now the company (which, provided the procedure is managed correctly, will not be an EU resident), the directive will not apply. The EU resident individual investor will receive dividends from the company, not interest, and so the directive will not apply at either stage.

Another possibility to explore is the use of redeemable preference shares, giving a return that, while commercially equivalent to a bank deposit, is legally a dividend (to which the directive does not apply).

It therefore appears that the EU savings directive will significantly restrict tax competition and make it less effective in the field of bank deposits and bonds, currently the area where competition is most fierce. This will be done either through a reduction in the number of territories free to engage in tax competition for this sector or through additional costs as providers explore ways around the new rules. Tax competition would survive, and continue to bring benefits to society at large, but these would be reduced by the increased costs and restricted opportunities for capital to benefit from low-tax jurisdictions.

The precise outcome, however, will depend on how it is interpreted and implemented; since the primary role of the European Court of Justice appears to be to advance European integration (rather than to determine the meaning of new laws), there is a real danger that future disputes over the application of the directive will see a widening of its scope, and a reduction in the opportunities for avoidance, by the court.

9 ATTACKS ON TAX COMPETITION II – THE OECD

Introduction

The Organisation for Economic Cooperation and Development (OECD) is a voluntary body whose members are the governments of the leading industrialised countries, primarily countries from Europe as well as the USA and Canada, Japan, Australia and New Zealand. Its aim, when founded in 1960, was to strengthen economic prosperity and therefore 'individual liberty and the increase in general well-being' (OECD Convention).

The OECD has always been at the forefront of support for global trade, and in tax matters it has done much to encourage the efficient operation of global free markets. Previously its main work in the tax field has been the development and encouragement of bilateral 'tax treaties' between members and other states. As mentioned in Chapter 6, the aim of these was to encourage cross-border trade and investment by removing tax barriers such as discriminatory taxation or double taxation (for example, where income from capital suffers full tax both in the investor's home country and in the country in which he invests). This was essential in the post-war climate: even today, after the reductions in taxation of investment income in the 1980s, if an investor suffers 40 per cent taxation in two countries on the same income there will be little left.

This beneficial work is still continuing: for example, the OECD has helped to settle the tax treatment of electronic commerce, where disagreements about the legal nature of electronically delivered goods and services risked the re-emergence of the problems of double taxation. It has also been seeking, however, to act against tax competition, prompted by some of its member governments (particularly those in western Europe).

This drive, the OECD's 'Harmful Tax Practices' initiative, began in 1996 and came to prominence two years later with the publication of *Harmful Tax Competition: An emerging global issue* (OECD, 1998). Despite recognising that tax competition had been helpful in countering excessive tax rates in the post-war era, the OECD's stated objective in the report was: 'to counter the distorting effects of harmful tax competition ... and the consequences for national tax bases' (ibid., 1998), and the underlying motivation was clearly 'the consequences for national tax bases', the fear by the member governments (particularly those in the EU) of reduced and reducing tax revenues.

The OECD has therefore abandoned its commitment to global free markets, 'individual liberty and the increase in general well-being': where these conflict with the interests of governments they are to be suppressed.

The main action in support of these new anti-market aims was the drawing up of a list of tax havens, which were to be subjected to pressure to mend their ways under threat of a range of tax-related sanctions (primarily a denial of deduction for payments by member country taxpayers to tax haven entities, or at least a reversal of the burden of proof in such cases) and, should that be thought insufficient, further unspecified 'non-tax measures' (punitive sanctions).

Operation of the initiative

The OECD has no legal powers or enforcement mechanisms, either against its members (the major developed economies) or, particularly, against non-member governments. The initiative was, however, a clear proposal to threaten non-members into complying; its objective was to: 'enable Member countries to coordinate their responses to the problems posed by tax havens and to encourage these jurisdictions to re-examine their policies' (ibid.).

Negotiation with non-member tax havens, the production of a list of those that did not cooperate and the introduction of sanctions against them were to be the main external acts of the initiative. There is also a self-review of their own harmful tax practices by member states and non-binding procedures for them to be removed.

The OECD appeared to have been alert to the political problems of the world's major economies being seen to threaten smaller states, and considerable efforts were made to try to present the initiative as being objective. Part of this was the adoption of a legalistic framework, attempting to define 'harmful tax competition' in the hope that any sanctions imposed would be seen as having an equitable basis. In the 1998 report, therefore, a 'harmful preferential tax regime' is defined as having 'a low or zero effective tax rate' and one or more of:

- no or low effective tax rates;
- 'ring fencing' of regimes;
- lack of transparency;
- lack of effective exchange of information. (ibid.)

Ignoring the double counting of low effective tax rates, which somehow was left in as one of the possible factors as well as being the primary test (in a possible attempt at clarification, the 2001 report refers to no or low effective tax rates as a 'gateway criterion'), there were still several ways in which a country could be defined as a tax haven.

The OECD was also concerned to ensure, however, that there was no escape for tax havens that tried to change their laws to avoid the definition. There was therefore also a range of secondary factors that 'can assist in identifying harmful preferential regimes':

- an artificial definition of the tax base;
- failure to adhere to international transfer pricing principles;
- foreign source income exempt from residence country tax;
- negotiable tax rate or tax base;
- existence of secrecy provisions;
- access to a wide network of tax treaties;
- regimes that are promoted as tax minimisation vehicles;
- the regime encourages purely tax-driven operations or arrangements. (ibid.)

It is not always clear what these are meant to add to the definition: the first four seem just to be examples of a low or zero effective tax rate, and the fifth simply another way of saying 'lack of effective exchange of information'. The seventh is also ambiguous, referring to promotion 'with the acquiescence of' the country in question; this could refer to the use of the regime by independent tax advisers which is not actively suppressed. The intention, however, is clearly to widen the scope of the definition to ensure that no tax havens can escape being classified as engaging in harmful tax competition. The last two in particular were clearly catch-all provisions designed to ensure that no effective tax haven could escape the net.

Similarly, the drafting of the 1998 report leaves it unclear as to how these eight secondary indicators are to be used. It is not stated whether their presence can make a tax system preferential even in the absence of the main indicators, or alternatively whether to be a harmful preferential tax regime a system would have to qualify under the main indicators and also show some of the secondary signs. Parts of the 1998 report (e.g. paras. 60 and 68) suggest the former approach, others (e.g. para. 59) suggest the latter; the 2001 report glosses over this issue, mentioning the secondary indicators only in passing. The overall approach of the initiative, however, is to define harmful tax regimes in as wide a manner as possible, which suggests that the secondary indicators are intended to bring tax systems into the definition by their presence rather than exclude them by their absence.

Failure of the initiative – the 'level playing field'

The OECD's attempt to protect its members' tax revenues by suppressing tax havens has, despite generating a great deal of heat and comment, largely failed (at least on its own terms). It remains a risk, however – less that it might be fully implemented than that some of the proposals for partial implementation may seriously damage the effectiveness of tax competition.

Much of the credit for the OECD's failure must go to campaigners in the USA (mainly under the umbrella of the Coalition for Tax Competition) and the Caribbean (notably Sir Ronald Sanders of Antigua and Barbuda). Their work is little acknowledged, however, as the OECD persists, for political reasons, in claiming that its initiative has been successful, and there is a considerable tactical advantage for the tax havens in allowing this misinformation to continue!

Clearly the initiative can only be a complete success if all tax havens are eradicated, otherwise tax avoidance will continue from the remaining havens. Fortunately five states are still refusing outright to cooperate (there were six, but Nauru was accepted as cooperating in December 2003). These five include three in mainland Europe (Andorra, Liechtenstein and Monaco), which seriously damages the success of the initiative. This still leaves the major offshore tax havens promising to comply, however, which will at least seriously weaken tax competition by reducing the number of competing players and, by removing some of the most efficient operators, adding to the costs of tax avoidance.

In addition, even though the OECD claims that the remaining identified tax havens have agreed to cooperate by signing 'commitment letters', it is hoped that many of these are almost meaningless. Most tax havens have attached riders to their commitment letters that make conformity with the OECD guidelines conditional on all other nations, including the OECD member states themselves, being subjected to them and the related sanctions. As an example, the letter signed by Antigua and Barbuda includes the following pre-condition:

> Those jurisdictions, including OECD Member countries
> and other countries and jurisdictions yet to be identified,
> that fail to make equivalent commitments or to satisfy the
> standards of the 1998 Tax Competition Report, will be the
> subject of a framework of co-ordinated defensive measures.

This has been accepted by the OECD, and in return it has agreed that countries that issue commitments including such wording will not be subjected to sanctions under the Harmful Tax Practices initiative. In other words, the tax havens (and most of them included a similar condition) will not have to follow the OECD guidelines until all countries, including the OECD members, are forced to do likewise.

By inserting these pre-conditions, tax haven governments executed a shrewd political step, as it would have been highly damaging for the OECD members to refuse such provisos and so to be seen publicly insisting on small, often poor, nations accepting restrictions that they were not prepared to be subjected to themselves.

These riders would not be a serious weakness if there had been a tight definition of harmful tax practices. As discussed above, however, the OECD began the process with a very wide definition that is potentially applicable to a wide range of aspects of member nations' tax regimes. Coupled with the lack of any effective judicial mechanism to determine whether a particular tax regime is harmful, this all-encompassing definition will mean that any threat of further action against the havens can be easily challenged by pointing to practices in member countries.

To demonstrate the extent of this issue, Table 6 shows the status of each of the OECD's initial target countries, according to the commitment letters posted on the OECD's website. A mere six states were pressured into signing unconditional commitment letters, and a further six entered into early 'preliminary agreements' on what they hoped were favourable terms. Four others persuaded the OECD that they are not tax havens, including, astonishingly, Barbados (discussed in more detail below),

Table 6 **Status of the OECD's initial target countries**

	Unconditional commitment	Preliminary agreement	Conditional agreement	Non-haven	No agreement
Andorra					•
Anguilla			•		
Antigua			•		
Aruba			•		
Bahamas			•		
Bahrain	•				
Barbados				•	
Belize			•		
Bermuda		•			
British V.I.	•				
Cayman Islands		•			
Cook Islands			•		
Cyprus		•			
Dominica	•				
Gibraltar			•		
Grenada			•		
Guernsey			•		
Isle of Man			•		
Jersey			•		
Liberia					•
Liechtenstein					•
Maldives				•	
Malta		•			
Marshall Islands					•
Mauritius		•			
Monaco					•
Montserrat			•		
Nauru			•		
Neth. Antilles	•				
Niue			•		
Panama			•		
Samoa			•		
San Marino		•			
Seychelles			•		
St Kitts & Nevis	•				
St Lucia	•				
St Vincent			•		
Tonga				•	
Turks & Caicos			•		
US Virgin Islands				•	
Vanuatu			•		

described by a tax planning manual (Azzara) as 'a responsible, low-tax haven' offering 'many of the prime tax haven attributes'.

To understand the strength of the reciprocity clauses, it is necessary to examine the definition of a 'harmful tax practice' under the OECD initiative. As discussed above, this definition was being pulled in two directions: a presentational desire to appear objective and a practical need to prevent tax havens from moving themselves outside the definition. This resulted in a neutral legal-istic definition that was still wide enough to catch any potential tax haven activity.

In order to prevent any potential tax havens slipping through its net, the OECD has produced an extremely wide definition (particularly if the eight secondary indicators can be used in the absence of the main tests). This was presumably thought to be essential to avoid the earlier problems where tax authorities seemed to be engaged in an unending 'fire-fighting' exercise, constantly blocking the loopholes that the tax avoidance industry continually finds in their previous legislation. The recent UK provisions on 'designer rates' of tax are a case in point: earlier CFC (controlled foreign companies) legislation had been triggered by a haven having tax rates below a certain level, but tax havens responded by allowing companies to choose their own tax rates so that they paid less tax but not so much less that they triggered the anti-avoidance legislation in their home countries.

The problem with this approach for the OECD was that it was impossible to catch all the 'traditional' tax havens without also including a large number of attributes of member states' own tax systems. It is therefore this wide definition of harmful tax practices which has given force to the tax havens' main weapon against their plans. As we have seen, most of the tax havens on the

OECD's target list have gained exemption from sanctions without any need to alter their systems by the use of a reciprocity clause in their commitment letters, under which their compliance is conditional on sanctions being applied to all nations (including OECD members) which have aspects of their tax systems that fall within the definition of a harmful tax regime. While this may not initially seem to be a valuable clause, the very width of the 1998 report's definition gives it teeth; with such a loose definition it seems that all OECD member countries will have to be subjected to sanctions (or dismantle valued parts of their own tax regimes) before pressure can be brought to bear on the smaller recalcitrant states.

The European tax-advantaged regimes are well known to all in the tax-avoidance industry, and it is not surprising that many would fall within the original OECD definition, primarily by offering low effective tax rates and being ring-fenced. These come in a bewildering variety. The most obvious is the Luxembourg 1929 corporation (a tax-exempt holding company), but there are many others, some of which are hidden within the detail of the relevant country's tax legislation.

The International Financial Services Centre regime in the Republic of Ireland (now condemned by the European Union but previously popular for internal group financing companies) and the Canary Islands tax regime operated by Spain (and Portugal's similar scheme in Madeira) are some of the best known in the industry, all of which are ring-fenced low effective tax regimes.

A less obvious form of tax competition is offered by Belgium in the form of its 'coordination centre' regime, a tax exemption for head office functions of multinational groups, which not only gives a ring-fenced low effective tax rate but also meets the OECD secondary indicators of an artificial definition of the tax base and failure to adhere to international transfer pricing principles, as it operates by permitting profits to be calculated on an unrealistic mark-up basis. It is very common for European countries to operate in this way: Denmark recently introduced a similar system, and while the UK does not explicitly offer such a service it nevertheless ensures that its tax system overall makes it an attractive location for the parent headquarters of multinational companies. The benefit to the country concerned is less in the actual situation of the head office than in the associated wealth from directors and attendant high-value employment.

An even better hidden example, which does not even show up in an examination of the country's tax legislation, is the highly cooperative attitude of some tax authorities in their negotiation of advance pricing arrangements. Under this, the authorities will negotiate with multinational groups considering locating in their country, effectively allowing them to agree an artificial method by which their profits will be calculated. In addition to giving a low effective tax rate, this also meets almost the full set of the OECD's secondary indicators: an artificial definition of the tax base, failure to adhere to international transfer pricing principles, a negotiable tax base, access to a wide range of tax treaties, regimes that are promoted as tax minimisation vehicles, and encouragement of purely tax-driven operations or arrangements. In the 1990s the Netherlands was notorious within the tax profession for this type of activity.

An associated benefit of using the Netherlands is its highly cooperative attitude towards its associated tax haven, the Netherlands Antilles. The use of group tax haven finance companies has already been discussed in Chapter 6, but in practice such companies are less effective than they should be because high-tax countries will impose withholding taxes on the interest paid to the tax haven finance company. In contrast the Netherlands has a tax treaty with the Netherlands Antilles under which no withholding tax will be levied, making the Netherlands Antilles a very attractive location for a group finance company. The Netherlands benefits not only indirectly but also by insisting that a small percentage of the interest stays in the Netherlands as it is flowed through to the tax haven.

The regime that has attracted the most attention in Europe is the Luxembourg withholding tax exemption. This was a key factor in Germany's pressure for a European Union minimum with-holding tax (see Chapter 8: Luxembourg is thought to be a major recipient of the massive capital outflow following Germany's intro-duction of withholding taxes on interest), and as its commercial success results from its combination of a low effective tax rate and a lack of effective exchange of information, it is clearly a harmful tax practice under the OECD's definition.

Luxembourg is one of the two OECD member countries that abstained from the 1998 report, but it is difficult to see the other members imposing serious sanctions against it in order to force a change of regime, even with such sanctions being a pre-condition for cooperation by non-member countries. Indeed, the imposition of sanctions against Luxembourg would be impossible for most OECD members, owing to their obligations (such as the guarantee of free movement of goods, capital and services and various non-discrimination provisions) under their common membership of the European Union.

It is not just the smaller European states which engage in this type of activity: the UK's tax system is not above criticism either. The exemption from taxation for the overseas income of resident but non-domiciled individuals (explained above) is the most frequently quoted example, being a harmful tax measure under the 1998 report owing to its zero effective rate and ring-fencing. Even though the practice is available to residents it does not apply to UK nationals, and so still falls within the 1998 report's very wide definition of ring-fencing, being 'partly insulated from the domestic market'.

If the secondary indicators are applied to the UK then there are many aspects of its tax system that should be classed as harmful tax practices. Examples include the incredibly high taper relief on capital gains tax (under which 75 per cent of the gain can be tax free), which is arguably an 'artificial definition of the tax base', as are some of the enhanced capital allowances (deductions of up to 100 per cent of capital expenditure are allowed in the year of purchase, even though for accounts purposes the cost will be spread over a number of years), and the shipping tonnage tax (under which shipping businesses can be taxed at a flat rate rather than as a percentage of their profits – a measure specifically designed to attract overseas capital investment). These are not merely accidental. Former Chancellor Nigel Lawson admitted in his autobiography that the Enterprise Zone allowance (which allows taxable profits to be dramatically reduced by giving noncommercial depreciation rates on the cost of building a factory) was 'directly promoted as a tax minimisation vehicle' during negotiations surrounding Nissan's car factory near Sunderland.

The OECD could not ignore all these tax haven attributes in its own members, and so its 2000 report listed 47 'potentially harmful' tax regimes in its 29 member countries. Of the brief sample of regimes described above, the following were included:

- Luxembourg 1929 corporation;
- Belgian coordination regime;
- Netherlands Cost-plus Ruling and Intra-group Finance Activities;
- Ireland International Financial Services Centre.

These are, of course, some of the most blatantly haven-style regimes within the OECD. A number of regimes, however, were not included in the OECD's list:

- Canary Islands tax regime operated by Spain;
- Luxembourg withholding tax exemptions;
- All the UK regimes mentioned above.

Indeed, the UK was described as one of only eight OECD member countries that apparently do not have any tax regimes that are even potentially within the scope of the initiative. It may be an indication of the different attitude to old and new members that Hungary (which joined the OECD in 1996) was listed for its Venture Capital Companies whereas the UK (original 1961 member) was not listed for its Venture Capital Trust, a type of investment holding company in which not only the company itself but also its shareholders are exempt from tax on dividends and capital gains. The USA does have one regime included, but this is the Foreign Sales Corporation (which was already at the time likely to be abolished under challenge from the WTO), rather than its tax exemption for interest payments to non-residents.

The identification of these regimes would not have been a problem under the processes as envisaged in the 1998 report, as their removal or continuation would have been by negotiation between the members, each of which would have its own relevant regimes to bring to a trade-off. Indeed, the limited range of regimes included possibly reflects the process for OECD member states, which was based on self-review as opposed to the external review imposed on non-members. What has changed is that the reciprocity clauses insisted on by many of the small tax haven nations could well bring these member regimes to the forefront. If small non-member havens have been granted immunity from sanctions by the OECD unless member countries are also subjected to them for breaches of the same rules, then the applicability or otherwise of the 1998 definitions to many long-standing provisions of OECD member nations' tax systems will become a crucial issue.

A final weakness of the OECD's position, especially given the likelihood of disagreement about the applicability of the definition to particular provisions, is its lack of an independent and accepted (or indeed any) judicial arm. Currently the only body able to judge such issues is an international forum, which is likely to result in all submissions degenerating into political rather than legal argument. There will be no body able to issue a binding judgement (or even a judgement with sufficient independence to be generally accepted), and so any sanctions can be met by a charge of favouritism.

In short the OECD's future action is liable to be severely hampered by its own device. It presumably opted for a wide definition of harmful tax practices to prevent tax havens from slipping through its net. Once the havens gained acceptance for the reciprocity clauses in their commitment letters, however, this strength became a weakness. The OECD will be prevented from imposing sanctions against flagrant tax havens unless it also forces its own members to repeal provisions that they will themselves regard as beneficial.

Pre-ordained failure?

In establishing why the OECD's initiative failed, it is useful to draw a distinction between external events that would have led to failure of a potentially successful programme and internal weaknesses that doomed it from the start. There are several reasons why the initiative failed, and it was indeed affected by external events, but in general it was always unlikely to succeed against determined opposition.

As discussed above, the initiative had to be a global one. A single functioning tax haven would be enough to enable tax competition, albeit in a weakened form, to survive. This made it a challenging target right from the start, even given that the initiative began badly, with two OECD members, Luxembourg and Switzerland, abstaining from the 1998 report. If only one functioning tax haven would bring about failure, the existence of two should have made the whole process a non-starter, and especially these two, as they are both well established and trusted, with modern infrastructure and good communications, and above all likely to be protected, as a result of their member status, from OECD sanctions.

Presumably the other members thought that pressure could eventually be brought to bear on their co-members, as the European Union is trying through its proposed Savings Tax Directive, but subsequently a further two member governments abstained from the follow-up 2001 report: Belgium and Portugal. Their reasons were not given, but both have tax regimes that potentially fall within the OECD definition of harmful tax competition. Although not thought of as classic tax havens, Belgium has a long-established special regime for 'coordination' centres for international groups, and Portugal has tax regimes developed by the autonomous region of Madeira.

A second internal problem is the OECD's complete lack of jurisdiction. As it is a voluntary inter-governmental organisation rather than a supra-national federal government it has no legislative or executive force over either its own members or outsiders. The intention was to impose its will by sanctions, but these would be effective only if its members agreed to implement them. Given that four members have now disassociated themselves from the process, and that many of the target tax havens were client states of members and therefore likely to be protected, it was always going to be difficult to make sanctions watertight. It is not surprising that one of the five remaining states that have refused any degree of cooperation is Liechtenstein, which is closely protected by OECD member Switzerland. Indeed, it is sad that the UK has not thought it worthwhile to give better support to its associated territories, particularly given the related financial and legal work that flows into London from taxpayers taking advantage of jurisdictions such as the Channel Islands and the Caribbean tax havens.

It could, however, have been a reasonable assumption that sufficient force could be brought to bear on non-members to severely restrict tax haven activity until the major external event that effectively brought an end to the initiative as first conceived: the change of government in the USA. The committed involvement of the USA, as the world's largest economy, and a close geographical neighbour of many tax havens, in any series of sanctions against the havens was crucial and, under the Clinton administration, seemed assured. The election of George W. Bush to the presidency and a concerted lobbying campaign by opponents of the OECD initiative appear to have brought about at least a weakening in US support, and it seems increasingly unlikely that any effective sanctions will be brought to bear in the near future. The re-election of the Bush administration in November 2004, and the strengthening of its support in Congress, is likely to weaken the OECD's tax competition initiative still more. This may even go farther than lack of cooperation with any proposed sanctions. In 2004 the US Senate called for a withdrawal of all funding from the OECD unless it drops its Harmful Tax Practices initiative (a serious threat, as the USA contributes a quarter of the OECD's funding).

The final problem, which should have been expected but apparently wasn't, was the concerted opposition of the tax havens themselves. Presumably the OECD thought that they could pick off uncooperative states one by one, and indeed if they had been opposed only by the current non-European signatories (Liberia and the Marshall Islands) it might still have been possible to bring effective pressure to bear. Instead, however, the havens presented an almost unanimous front, with most refusing to sign commitment letters unless they were emasculated by the pre-condition of global enforcement referred to above.

A change of tack

Faced from without by concerted opposition, and from within by open dissent from four members and waning enthusiasm from the most important, the OECD has backtracked and granted immunity from sanctions on the basis of these near-meaningless conditional commitments.

It has also watered down its definition of its targets. To repeat, in the 1998 report a 'harmful preferential tax regime' is defined as having: 'a low or zero effective tax rate' and one or more of:

- no or low effective tax rates;
- 'ring fencing' of regimes;
- lack of transparency;
- lack of effective exchange of information.

There is also the range of secondary factors that extend the scope and 'can assist in identifying harmful preferential regimes' (see above). Clearly the overall approach of the 1998 report was to define harmful tax regimes in as wide a manner as possible.

There are therefore numerous ways in which a tax system could be brought within the scope of the 1998 report. The OECD has, however, managed to present its limited success of five 'unco-operative' nations only by drastically restricting its target. Several states that were initially included on the list of tax havens potentially subject to sanctions have been removed on the grounds that they have adequate information-sharing agreements: for example, Barbados was given immunity from pressure to reform because it had, according to the OECD announcement, 'long-standing information exchange arrangements with other countries, which are found by its treaty partners to operate in an effective manner', and it 'is also willing to enter into tax information exchange arrangements with those OECD Member countries with which it currently does not have such arrangements' (OECD, 2001b).

Note that there is no mention of ring-fencing of regimes.

According to the 1998 report this, coupled with low effective rates, is sufficient to identify a nation as a tax haven, but this has been quietly dropped by the OECD in order to give a semblance of success (on the grounds that it is too difficult to determine whether it is present). Alternatively a tax haven could be identified by lack of transparency. This is indeed covered in the joint press release, but only by the unsupported statement that: 'Barbados has in place established procedures with respect to transparency' (ibid.).

The contrast with the information exchange approach is clear: there is no statement that the transparency procedures actually work to prevent hidden ownership, or even that they are designed to do so (indeed, it would be semantically correct to state that Switzerland has 'established procedures with respect to transparency', even though they are designed to prevent rather than enhance transparency).

It therefore appears that, of the several ways of identifying a tax haven in its 1998 report, the OECD has subsequently ignored ring-fencing and all the secondary signs and has fudged transparency. The only remaining tests out of a once comprehensive definition are low effective rates and information exchange. This may indeed be a useful goal for the tax authorities of the OECD member countries (although a highly limited one without effective transparency provisions), but it is hardly the great assault on tax havens that was initially planned.

Although the 2000 report states that 'the project is not primarily about collecting taxes', this restriction of the definition of a harmful tax practice shows that this is really the only aim. It seems clear that, in the light of opposition from within and without, the OECD has been forced to emasculate its scheme to be able to claim success.

Continuing danger

So the OECD's initiative against tax competition may appear to have run into the sand, thanks to the concerted action by the tax havens. There are, however, still risks arising from the concentration on information exchange.

It appears that the OECD is now concentrating merely on forcing low-tax jurisdictions to provide extensive information to the tax authorities in its member high-tax jurisdictions, to enable them to collect taxes from their residents. This will under current laws still permit many forms of tax avoidance to take place, including the use of offshore associated companies to provide group finance or hold group intellectual property, and the use of offshore investments by those who are not subject to worldwide taxation in their state of residence (such as non-domiciled UK residents).

This approach, however, if successful, will seriously restrict the operation of tax competition in other areas. It will also leave tax competition highly vulnerable to future changes in the law: a tightening of Controlled Foreign Companies legislation, for example, could see the European governments attempting to bring far more offshore companies into their tax net.

Tax competition would therefore be far less efficient if there were a system of full information sharing. Not only would potential future benefits be lost, but if governments can efficiently tax investments in tax havens then it would also be possible for them to reverse the beneficial tax changes of the last couple of decades without risking a loss of their tax base to tax havens. Wider society, as well as those companies and individuals that directly benefit from tax havens, could therefore lose the benefits that tax competition has already brought.

In addition, this narrowing of the scope of the OECD initiative may make it easier for it to satisfy the 'level playing field' clauses in the conditional cooperation agreements signed by most of the traditional tax havens. Under the full definition the OECD members have many tax haven attributes that they are unwilling to abolish, but most of them already have extensive information-sharing agreements between each other's tax authorities, and so could easily satisfy the requirements of a reduced definition.

Tax havens, and those OECD members that value financial freedom and a drive towards low taxes, should therefore resist information sharing just as they have resisted other aspects of the OECD initiative. It is hardly an equal process; as the traditional tax havens have no need for information from other tax authorities it will be effectively a one-way street. Enforced information sharing is just as much a restriction on tax competition as any other aims of the OECD.

It may appear to be a high-risk strategy, but instead of welcoming the narrowing of the OECD's focus on information sharing only, the traditional tax havens should insist that it is implemented in full or not at all. Only in that way can they obtain the full value of their 'level playing field' clauses by pointing to 'harmful tax practices' in OECD member jurisdictions and insisting that any sanctions be imposed equally.

10 ATTACKS ON TAX COMPETITION III
   – VALUE ADDED TAX

Introduction

The debate about tax competition generally focuses on the taxation of capital, and the effects on the supposedly less mobile labour. This is to ignore, however, a substantial part of the tax system – consumption taxes. As seen above (Chapter 4), across the EU consumption taxes account for 28 per cent of government revenue, more than taxes on capital, and so competition in respect of consumption taxes is also important.

Consumption taxes are levied on individuals when they buy goods or services. Value Added Tax (VAT), the main consumption tax in the EU, is a broadly based tax that covers nearly all goods and services (although in the UK a relatively large number of items, such as children's clothes and food, are VAT free). Initially consumption taxes were levied on all purchases within the country (collected by the supplier) and on all imports (collected by customs officers at the point of entry into the country), except for very small 'duty-free' allowances for travellers, but this was modified by the EU's single market.

VAT in cross-border trade

Being largely a product of the post-war era, the VAT system in the

EU often struggles to adapt to modern business activity, particularly cross-border trade.

Theoretically there are two main options for charging VAT on international activities, giving taxing rights to either the country where the supplier is based (the 'origin system') or that of the country where the customer is based (the 'destination system'). This could lead to either double taxation (where the supplier is located in a country that uses the destination system and the customer in a country that operates the origin system), or non-taxation (vice versa). In practice, however, this is unlikely, as VAT and similar taxes generally all use the destination system for the bulk of transactions. This common approach is not particularly a result of coordination (although it is the method adopted by the IMF's model tax code), but is merely a reflection of the purpose of VAT – as a consumption tax, it is more logical for tax to be levied where the consumption takes place, presumably in most cases the country of residence of the consumer. This approach has been accepted by the World Trade Organization (WTO). In response to complaints by the USA against the EU, the WTO accepted that the consumption tax nature of VAT meant that it was legitimate for EU governments not to charge VAT on exports (although it was not acceptable for the USA to exempt companies from profits-based taxes on their overseas business).

This approach severely limits the opportunities for tax competition in the VAT field. Under the destination system the consumer's home-country VAT system will be applied to all purchases, and so the same tax will be payable wherever the supplier is based.

Despite this, there is scope for some tax competition in VAT because the destination system is not used exclusively. This is largely because of practical problems of collection. VAT and related taxes rely on the supplier to charge and pay VAT (which eases the task of collection for the tax authorities by reducing the number of taxpayers to monitor). This is difficult in a cross-border context, because the customer's home tax authority is unlikely to have either the legal jurisdiction or the practical ability to enforce taxes against a foreign resident supplier.

For transactions between an EU and a non-EU country, the EU's VAT approach is to operate the theoretically pure destination system for goods, as the tax can be collected at the point of entry along with customs duties. The only exceptions from this are strictly limited personal imports (the old 'duty-free allowance'), and a *de minimis* that allows retail imports below a low level (currently £36) to escape VAT. Although small, this latter exemption has been exploited, particularly by the Channel Islands, where the cut-flower industry is able to make VAT-free sales directly to UK consumers. Recently the music industry has also attempted to exploit this provision, making online CD sales from the Channel Islands. Packages must be below the limit (if above, then VAT is charged on the full amount), and the benefit will be reduced by increased delivery charges. There is still sufficient activity to concern governments, however, and a series of amendments to the basic position have been authorised by the Council to prevent 'loss in revenue'. For example, in 2005 Denmark was permitted to suspend a *de minimis* of €10 on 'certain magazines' imported from outside the EU, because publishers were 're-routing the distribution of their publications to subscribers in Denmark via territories [outside the EU]'; the avoidance of VAT even on such a low cover price was felt to be sufficient to justify delivery charges via a non-EU country, and the cumulative effect was feared to be large enough to prompt the Danish government to seek permission to change the law (Council Decision 2005/258/EC).

For services, the position is slightly more complex owing to the difficulty of collecting VAT where there is no physical product crossing the border. The default position is therefore that services are charged on the origin principle (i.e. the supplier's place of business). This therefore gives opportunities for tax competition. Businesses based in countries that do not charge VAT or any equivalent (or which operate on a pure destination principle basis) can make sales of services to EU customers without VAT either in the country of supply or the country of destination. It would also put EU-based suppliers at a competitive disadvantage, because they would have to charge VAT on exports to customers who either did not pay VAT in their own country, or who would have to pay again if their home country operated the destination principle.

In practice, however, this opportunity is limited, because the EU operates a destination principle for those services in which governments believe there is widespread scope for tax competition. The specific case of electronic commerce is discussed in more detail below, but for a specific range of business-to-business services (for example, professional services, equipment leasing and telecoms) VAT has long been charged under the destination principle. There is therefore still scope for tax competition in VAT for the supply of services, either to non-business customers or (when to business customers) of services of a type that fall outside the destination principle rules, but the opportunity for changing behaviour is limited by the practical difficulties.

Electronic commerce

The system faced new challenges with the growth of the Internet and electronic shopping. This brought two problems for EU tax collectors. First, it made it far easier for individuals to contact sellers from other countries and buy goods from them. This led to a great increase in the volume of small packages of goods coming into the country through the postal systems. Charging VAT on purchases from outside the EU relies on customs officers stopping the goods at the point of entry, which is relatively easy for large commercial consignments but practically impossible with millions of small packages. Second, it became much easier to buy intangibles from other countries, such as downloaded software or music. It is difficult to stop a CD containing computer software coming into the country; it is impossible to do so if the same software is downloaded electronically. The EU therefore faced a challenge from loss of VAT revenue and put its domestic high-tech industry (which would have to charge VAT) at a disadvantage against non-EU competitors.[1] This was a serious concern to some businesses. The UK-based Internet service provider Freeserve launched legal challenges against the UK government because it had to charge VAT whereas its US competitor AOL did not.

The EU considered various options, including collecting the tax directly from the customer (practically impossible and very expensive), a moratorium on all Internet VAT in order to protect domestic businesses (supported by the UK, where most EU high-tech businesses are based, but opposed by all other governments) and a system where the credit card companies would collect VAT

---

1   This situation is economically equivalent to EU governments paying an import subsidy to firms exporting to the EU – it therefore causes economic welfare losses, ignoring any loss of tax revenue.

on all online sales (strongly opposed by the banks: not only would the costs have been high, but they generally do not have enough information about the goods or services bought to charge the correct amount).

In the end the EU chose the King Canute option. They widened the VAT charge on Internet purchases to cover foreign (non-EU) suppliers, and demanded that the supplier charge, collect and pay over the VAT just as an EU-based supplier would have to. The one flaw in the system is that the EU has no jurisdiction over non-EU businesses, and no way to enforce its tax demands. At the time the new rules were planned, the EU had hoped that the US government would agree to enforce these taxes against businesses in its territory. The USA has too much concern for the health of its businesses, however, to force them to act as unpaid tax collectors for the EU.

The new law is therefore highly unlikely to be obeyed, except by those multinational groups with assets in Europe that can be confiscated, and perhaps a few large companies that can be shamed into compliance. There is still therefore significant scope for tax competition in VAT for electronic commerce, particularly for small companies without any EU presence.

The single market

The above discussion concerns imports from outside (or exports to outside) the EU. For cross-border trading within the EU the situation is different, owing to the EU's desire to promote the single market and remove barriers to inter-member activity. This brings conflicts between the desire to promote the single market and the tax authorities' agenda of enforcing compliance and preventing tax competition.

These problems became prominent with the single market legislation of 1992, which opened up Europe's internal borders and allowed the free movement of goods throughout the EU. Effectively within the EU the 'origin principle' was to apply, so that the VAT charged depended on the location of the selling business, not the country of residence of the customer. This was intended to promote the single market by removing barriers to inter-member trading by businesses (under the destination principle the complications of dealing with multiple VAT systems depending on the customer's place of residence would be a serious administrative barrier, particularly for small businesses), but one consequence was that individuals in the EU became able to travel to other EU member states to make their purchases, pay the taxes of the country in which the purchase took place, and bring them back to their home country without paying any additional tax. Unlike the old system of 'duty-free allowances', still used for purchases made outside the EU, this new single market system puts no limit on the amount of imports, provided they are for personal use rather than resale.

Governments with high levels of VAT were worried about tax competition if their citizens could shop in lower-tax countries. This was a serious concern: not only did the high-tax countries face the loss of consumption tax revenues, but also their domestic businesses would lose custom to suppliers in lower-taxed countries, having a knock-on effect on profits tax and employment. The UK government has been less concerned, partly because its VAT rate is one of the lowest in Europe (at 17.5 per cent; only Luxembourg's 15 per cent is lower), but also because the only land border the UK has with another EU country is that between Northern Ireland and the Republic of Ireland – hence transport costs will reduce the opportunities for UK residents to take advantage of lower rates elsewhere.

For high-VAT countries, however, particularly those with extensive land borders with other, lower-taxed, member states, this tax competition was a serious concern. A compromise was therefore reached to restrict the single market: the ability to bring purchases back from other EU countries without paying tax on imports would apply only if the individual physically travelled to the other country, made the purchase in person and brought the goods home himself (known as 'personal import'). It was felt that this was unlikely to result in high levels of tax competition in relation to VAT, because the differentials were not generally great enough to make physical travel worthwhile (especially as 'big-ticket' items, such as cars, were excluded from the personal import regime).

The maximum VAT saving for most goods within the EU is 10 per cent (Sweden's 25 per cent against Luxembourg's 15 per cent), and it was thought unlikely that significant numbers of taxpayers would travel between countries for a 10 per cent VAT saving. There is of course a greater saving where some countries have reduced VAT rates for particular items. The EU has a harmonised list of VAT-exempt items, but countries were able to retain reduced rates, or even super-reduced rates such as the UK's 0 per cent rate, for a range of product types. This widens the potential VAT saving to 25 per cent. The European Commission has been trying to restrict the scope of reduced rates, limiting them to areas where there is a social policy justification, and it is now impossible to introduce new super-reduced rates (i.e. those below 5 per cent), and other reduced rates are restricted to certain categories of goods.

At first sight the scope for tax competition through reduced rates seems limited by the type of product subject to reduced rates; the possibility of a 6 per cent VAT rate for hairdressing in Luxembourg, or bicycle repairs in the Netherlands, does not appear likely to result in significant cross-border activity. The European Commission's report on the issue (COM(2001) 599 final), however, reveals some concern: 'French representatives of biscuit, chocolate and confectionery manufactures maintain that their products are suffering distortions of competition' (particularly from Luxembourg, where the rate is just 3 per cent) (ibid., note 14), and similar problems are reported concerning agricultural products. It is possible also that the UK's zero ratings could enable tax competition, particularly on medicines (where there is a growing international market over the Internet), food (subject to cultural differences), books and children's clothes.

There is fierce competition relating to consumption taxes within the EU, but only for those specific goods where there are other taxes charged at high rates, not for VAT. The UK government loses substantial amounts of revenue from cross-border purchases of alcohol and tobacco (estimated by Customs Associates Ltd for the European Commission at €400 million p.a. in 2001), because it has set excise duties on these items at rates far higher than those of neighbouring countries, so that it is highly profitable for British citizens to travel to France, Belgium or Spain to make these purchases (no longer France for tobacco, as the French government has progressively raised its duty levels, reducing the differential, though this seems to have been purely for domestic policy reasons). But even here there are thought to be geographical differences, with cross-border shopping much more prevalent on the south and east coasts of England near the

Channel ports. Similarly, in parts of France and Belgium there are now no petrol stations, because tax differentials make fuel in neighbouring Luxembourg so much cheaper that businesses cannot compete, but this is confined to a narrow geographical area.

If the customer does not physically travel to another EU country to make his purchases, but has them delivered, then the 'personal import' rules do not apply and the destination rather than the origin system is used. In these cases of 'distance selling', the customer will be charged his home rates of VAT (and other duties), wherever in the EU the supplier is located. This is costly for the business making the sales because, just as for domestic sales, it has to calculate and charge the correct rate of VAT. This means that businesses making deliveries to individual customers throughout the EU now have to deal with 25 VAT systems, theoretically the same but in practice subtly different. This removes the possibility of tax competition, because the same VAT will be charged wherever the supplier is based.

In this way the governments of the EU member states restricted the single market and the free movement of goods to protect themselves from effective consumption tax competition. The only way to take advantage of lower consumption taxes within the EU is to buy from a very small business (as these are exempt from the 'distance selling' rules and operate under the origin principle) or to physically travel to another country with either a lower general VAT rate or a specific reduced rate (in which case the costs and time would reduce any tax advantage). The only real scope for widespread consumption tax competition is therefore in relation to products with specific high taxes, such as alcohol, tobacco and petrol, which the Commission wants to harmonise anyway.

Conclusion

There is a possibility of effective consumption tax competition for taxpayers in the European Union, but only in limited areas (mainly those goods subject to high specific excise duties, and downloaded intangibles). As with the Savings Tax Directive, the other main area where the EU is trying to stop tax competition, its attempts to collect VAT on imports have so far largely failed because it does not have authority over the rest of the world. And as with savings tax it is mainly the USA which has the strength to hold out against EU demands.

There is still some scope for tax competition, either within the EU under the 'personal import' regime, or from outside the EU for either low-value goods or services that are outside the specific charging schemes. Although the scope is apparently small, the concern of EU governments suggests that tax competition in these areas remains significant. The most likely area for substantial activity is in the electronic commerce field, where the EU's rules to prevent tax competition are far from watertight.

11 ATTACKS ON TAX COMPETITION IV – OTHER EU ACTIVITY

Introduction

The EU Savings Directive is a direct attack on tax competition, in that it challenges the whole concept of countries' ability to set their own tax rates and benefit (or suffer) from the natural consequences of that decision.

In contrast other EU activity in the tax competition field is more subtle, and is capable of doing some good in that it corrects the natural tendencies of politicians to meddle with their tax systems to favour particular client groups. This 'corporate welfare', the state benefits given by politicians to particular industries, has recently started attracting more critical attention.

Clearly it is economically foolish for governments to tax successful businesses to fund unsuccessful ones: the successful activities will be loaded with too many burdens and their expansion will be hampered while unsuccessful businesses will expand beyond the point at which the cost of their activities is equal to the benefit. Sadly, however, corporate welfare remains popular, particularly because politicians insist on believing that they have a special insight that allows them to 'pick winners' that have 'unfairly' been denied funding by bankers and other financiers. Effectively this is another manifestation of the persistent belief in state planning. In addition it is another way in which politicians can divert resources to their client groups in the electorate, funding increased employment in their constituencies at the cost of slowing down the general economy.

State aid rules

The European Commission has, to its credit, taken action against this tendency. In recent years it has been extending this to tax systems. EU governments had generally stopped giving direct government grants (except where there are exemptions from the state aid rules), but they continued to pursue the same policy objectives through tax exemptions and reliefs targeted at particular industries or areas.

In 2001 the Commission began to use the state aid rules to stop tax breaks for specific business sectors. Its greatest achievement was the abolition of the Irish International Financial Services Centre (IFSC) regime. Under this system companies based in the Dublin docklands and operating in the financial services sector were subject only to a 10 per cent tax rate rather than the 30 per cent then levied on other Irish companies. This tax reduction proved very popular, and a flood of financial businesses (both group finance companies and retail investment management companies) moved to Dublin (incidentally fuelling a painful property boom). The advantage of Dublin was not just the low tax rate (other tax havens offered zero per cent) but also its geographical location, its educated workforce (including the returning diaspora) and the fact that other tax authorities around the world were slow to realise that Ireland was an effective tax haven, allowing activities there to escape investigation.

This last point was crucial. We saw earlier that businesses can set up finance companies based in tax havens to divert group profits to a low-tax environment, but that those profits cannot generally be paid out to the parent company (and hence out to the shareholders) as dividends without those dividends being taxed. In the UK tax system, as it then existed, it was briefly possible to pay dividends from an Irish finance subsidiary (subject to tax at only 10 per cent) up to a UK parent company (taxed at 30 per cent) without the UK company paying any tax (because Ireland was not classified as a tax haven).

The European Commission successfully argued that the Irish IFSC regime amounted to illegal state aid, because offering a tax reduction to a particular industry was effectively equivalent to a government grant to that industry. It also took similar action against other governments, including Spain's; Spanish coordination centres in the Basque region were allowed to calculate their taxable profits on a non-commercial basis so that although the headline tax rate was the same as for other companies their taxable profits, and hence their effective tax rate, were artificially low. Similar regimes in Belgium, France, Luxembourg and Germany were also targeted.

The effect of this was interesting, particularly in the case of Ireland. The Irish government replaced its special reduced 10 per cent rate of tax for particular industries with a general low tax rate of 12 per cent for all companies. As this was not targeted at specific industries it was immune from challenge under the state aid rules. Thanks to the initial success of the specific reduced rates in attracting business to the country, the Irish government was able to do this without significant loss of revenue.

The code of conduct

A further strand of the EU's moves against tax breaks for specific industries is its code of conduct for business taxation (negotiated by the 'Primarolo Group', named after the UK Treasury minister who chaired it).

This takes a wider approach, and looks at detailed provisions within member states' tax systems to see whether they act as distortionary influences on investment. A non-binding operation, the code was agreed in 1997 as part of a package of measures that included the Savings Tax Directive.

The group reported in 1999, and had as its basis a similar objective to the OECD's, to address 'those measures which affect, or may affect, in a significant way the location of business activity in the Community'. Member states were, however, keen to protect their independent authority to set their own tax rates, so (in contrast to the OECD's provisions) under the EU code of conduct measures were to be examined only if they led to 'a significantly lower effective level of taxation ... than those levels which generally apply in the Member State in question'. In other words it was a similar approach to the use of the state aid rules: member states were free to adopt general low levels of taxation, but not low rates (or low effective rates) for particular classes of business operations.

Again, because of the risk of simply moving tax avoidance outside the EU, the code was to be extended to associated and dependent territories of EU member states.

The group's report in 1999 identified 203 separate regimes that were potentially harmful within member states and a further 86 in the dependent and associated territories (including Sark, where the mere existence of the island seemed to be regarded as an abusive tax practice[1]).

The code was intended to then lead to a 'standstill and rollback' process, whereby, first, no new abusive regimes were to be introduced and then existing ones were to be progressively abolished (with a transitional period in which regimes were to be closed to new entrants but existing beneficiaries were allowed to continue).

The code of conduct has two of the problems associated with the OECD's action against its own members' tax exemptions: it is a voluntary process with no enforcement powers, and it is a political process with no objective judicial arm to decide what practices constitute harmful tax competition.

The European Court of Justice

As mentioned above, within the European Union direct taxes are the responsibility of the member states, not the Union. Just as member state governments must not allow their tax systems to breach the state aid rules, however, they must also not breach the 'fundamental freedoms' of the EU's founding treaty – the freedom of movement of people, goods and services, and capital.

The European Court of Justice (ECJ) sees itself as the guardian of these freedoms, and can declare national laws (including tax laws) to be invalid if they breach or improperly restrict these freedoms. It also interprets the freedoms very widely, and as a result in recent years it has struck down several provisions of member states' tax laws on the grounds that they discriminate against taxpayers who chose to exercise the fundamental freedoms.

---

1   Most of the jurisdictions had only specific aspects of their tax systems listed as being potentially harmful; Sark was treated as harmful in its entirety.

So far most of these court decisions relating to tax have concerned the freedom of movement of capital and the related freedom of business establishment, and so have struck down national tax provisions that seek to tax foreign-earned income (such as dividends received by a multinational group from its subsidiary companies in other member states) differently from domestic income. But there have also been cases concerning the freedom of movement of individuals, especially with regard to the taxation of cross-border commuters.

Although not specifically part of the tax competition debate, the actions of the ECJ represent another beneficial attempt by the EU to remove distortions and discrimination within the tax systems of its member states. They can also help strengthen tax competition within the European Union, as they remove barriers to relocation and therefore make it easier for taxpayers to benefit from lower tax rates elsewhere without being penalised by their home country. Their scope is limited, however, as the freedoms are valid only within the EU; thanks to the 'Fortress Europe' mentality, member states are still free to discriminate against taxpayers who try to take advantage of lower tax rates in non-EU countries.

Conclusion

Overall these initiatives are likely to be beneficial in removing hidden corporate welfare. They should therefore encourage the sort of tax reforms that the UK went through in the 1980s, leading towards a transparent, non-distortionary system that taxes a broad base (roughly equivalent to accounting profits) at a low rate rather than at a high headline rate with exemptions designed to encourage politically favoured types of business activity. It is these reformed tax systems which are least harmful to business activity and therefore least destructive of growth.

12 ATTACKS ON TAX COMPETITION V – OTHER ACTIVITY

World Trade Organization

In a similar way to the European Union's use of the state aid rules to block disguised subsidies for particular businesses, the World Trade Organization (WTO) has successfully attacked some distortionary tax exemptions offered by otherwise high-tax countries as being hidden export subsidies.

One of the major successes of the WTO was the European Union's claim that the USA's Foreign Sales Corporation regime, and its successor, the Extraterritorial Income Exclusion, amounted to export subsidies that were illegal under the WTO rules. Effectively this was an attempt by the USA to modify its residence-based tax system (see Chapter 6) to exempt certain types of overseas income earned by US residents (in particular corporations).

In much the same way as the Irish government responded to the European Commission's use of the state aid rules against its special 10 per cent rate of tax for International Financial Services Companies (see Chapter 11) by bringing in a general 12 per cent rate for all companies, there have been calls for the USA to respond to the WTO by switching entirely to a territorial tax system (under which it would make no attempt to tax any overseas income). As this would be a general rather than a targeted measure, and a fundamental aspect of its tax system rather than a specific exemption, it would be acceptable under WTO rules. There would, however, be problems with such a move, as it would make foreign investment more attractive than domestic investment for US residents.

In response the WTO has brought action against Belgium, France, Greece, Ireland and the Netherlands over aspects of their tax systems that it regards as amounting to export subsidies.

Like the European Commission's use of the state aid rules, this is potentially a beneficial process, preventing 'corporate welfare' disguised as tax provisions. There is a problem with the structure of the WTO disputes procedure, in that it is seen as being more of a political process than the European Court of Justice, but it is certainly more objective and better focused than the OECD processes.

United Nations

The United Nations (UN) has jumped on to the tax competition bandwagon, and has called for multinational activity to prevent 'capital flight'. There have even been calls for a UN commission to counter harmful tax competition.

Like many political discussions of tax competition, debate at the UN level is generally very simplistic. It concentrates on only half the picture (the transfer of investment capital to tax havens) and ignores the more valuable half (the efficient transfer back of capital to fund investments in non-haven countries).

On the back of the tax competition debate there have also been calls for some form of global tax, generally a self-interested attempt by the UN to increase its own resources. A common suggestion is a tax on financial transfers, attractive to many elements within the

UN as it attacks the whole basis of globalisation. This, however, would have serious negative consequences for world prosperity, as it would be a tax on economic activity rather than on profits. A study for the UN itself (McMahon, 2001)[1] described a global tax as 'unworkable, unnecessary and dangerous'.

The UN has also supported OECD calls for information exchange, and has its own tax package of desired innovations that includes a tax on migrants. Fortunately the structure of the United Nations makes it unlikely that any effective action will result.

Money laundering

One argument used by the opponents of tax havens is that they are used by criminals to hide the proceeds of their crime (money laundering). Indeed, after the September 11th attacks in the USA there was a brief campaign against tax competition on the grounds that tax havens assisted terrorist financing.

This contention has been disproved. It is true that regulation in tax havens is generally lower than in EU countries (this is another of their attractions), but this is because their regulation is better targeted, not because it does not exist. Offshore financial centres trade on their reputation, and they will soon lose custom from respectable investors if they are seen as being involved with criminals and terrorists.

The Financial Action Task Force of the OECD has accepted that tax havens are generally well regulated to prevent money laundering and terrorist financing. Indeed, studies have shown

---

1   Interestingly for a UN document, this study also drew on public choice theory in its rejection of the global tax, citing the lack of effective control over tax and spending decisions by the UN.

that the vast majority of criminal money is laundered not through tax havens but through London and New York, simply because the larger volumes of money passing through make it much more difficult for the authorities to spot individual transactions.

13 CONCLUSIONS

Tax competition is beneficial for all society

Tax competition has grown alongside the global free market as barriers to international trade, investment and labour mobility are reduced, so it becomes easier to take advantage of low taxes offered by different jurisdictions. Much of the opposition to tax competition is part of a wider opposition to global free markets, the desire to isolate a country (or, in the case of the EU, a block of countries) from the realities of the outside world. This protectionism, although attractive in the short term to some political groups, is damaging.

Tax competition brings various benefits, most obviously to those who take advantage of lower tax rates, but also to the wider community. By exposing countries to the consequences of high taxation (capital flight and lower labour productivity), tax competition acts as a check on governments' ability to raise taxes. If governments were perfectly wise, benevolent and competent then this would not necessarily be an advantage, but in reality it has several beneficial effects:

- It counters the tendency in modern politics for coalitions to gain support by taxing minorities to fund benefits for their client groups.

- Limiting taxation, and hence government funds, gives an incentive to governments to spend money more wisely. Effectively tax competition acts alongside the desire of voters for improved public services, forcing politicians to look for efficiency gains rather than increased taxation. These efficiencies can be practical (without tax competition governments have little incentive to control costs), but on a deeper level they can also encourage better choice of public projects, directing limited funds to those activities that are actually desired and valued by the electorate.
- If taxes on capital are too high, saving will be reduced; this reduces the available pool of capital for private sector investment and therefore results in lower (or less valuable) employment opportunities. The experience of the 1970s suggests that politicians need to be reminded of this by the spur of tax competition, otherwise, in a less open economy, investment can be stifled for too long and the economy seriously damaged.

The economic opposition to tax competition is based on the assumption that without tax competition governments would set tax rates at the optimum level and would spend the money raised perfectly efficiently. Opponents therefore ignore the advantages that tax competition brings, by assuming a perfect world. The feared 'race to the bottom', where tax competition would drive tax rates progressively down to zero, has clearly not happened, and in the real world the positive effects of tax competition appear to outweigh the negatives.

In addition, low-tax jurisdictions make global capital markets more efficient. Despite some valuable work by the OECD, national tax systems often do not fit together very well (particularly in the case of cross-border collective investment), risking double or treble taxation. Channelling money through low-tax jurisdictions ('tax havens') reduces this risk and so reduces barriers to cross-border investment that cooperation between governments has so far been unable to remove. As lower tax rates increase the available pool of investment capital, low-tax jurisdictions allow it to flow smoothly to the places where it will be most valuable.

Governments oppose tax competition

The main practical opposition to tax havens, that they attract an unfairly high proportion of global capital and therefore deprive European countries of needed investment, is therefore unsustainable. In reality low-tax jurisdictions act as conduits, allowing capital to flow around the world to the most suitable investment opportunities. The nature of tax havens is such that, in most cases, capital flows through them rather than stays in them to finance physical capital investment within the haven. The reality of business investment (for example, the need for developed infrastructure and proximity to markets) means that most of this investment capital will end up being directed back to the industrialised countries. Tax havens do not 'steal' global capital, but merely allow it to flow efficiently.

Governments, however, still oppose tax competition, not because it harms their citizens but because they resent restrictions on their own ability to raise funds. There are currently two main attacks on tax competition, both driven primarily by European governments.

- The European Union is trying to impose a minimum tax rate on bank interest, not just within its own borders but in various other countries on which it can put pressure (through geographical proximity or constitutional ties). This will attack what is currently one of the most effective areas of tax competition (bank deposits are highly mobile and can therefore take advantage of low taxes with very little cost), and will seriously damage the effectiveness of international capital markets.
- The Organisation for Economic Cooperation and Development (OECD) is trying to effectively abolish all serious tax competition, initially by closing down low-tax jurisdictions and latterly by putting serious barriers in the way of their effective use (through compulsory information exchange).

Both these initiatives are misguided attempts, mainly by high-tax, EU governments, to protect their own positions and allow them to continue to raise taxes while postponing the natural consequences of doing so in terms of reduced investment and employment.

Further initiatives in the European Union involve attempting to remove harmful internal tax competition, in the form not of reduced rates but of specific tax exemptions and related benefits for particular industries. To the extent that these exemptions constitute 'corporate welfare', a disguised attempt by politicians to subsidise favoured businesses at the expense of the general economy, the European Commission's moves to abolish these preferential regimes should be supported. It is this genuinely distortionary tax competition which is harmful, not the drive towards lower tax rates.

The effects of tax competition

The OECD accepts that tax competition helped remove various damaging aspects of tax systems that had grown up in the 1960s and 1970s.

The opposition to tax competition, primarily from EU governments, shows that it is still acting as a constraint on their tax-raising powers (otherwise they would not launch such wide-ranging campaigns to prevent it). As the main benefit of tax competition is its restraint on governments' ability to raise taxes, it works as long as they believe it does. Tax revenues are not falling in Europe, however; government revenues as a percentage of GDP are increasing. Nor is the tax burden on capital (probably the most mobile tax base and therefore the one where tax competition is likely to be strongest) decreasing.

So if governments accept that tax competition is an effective constraint on their tax-raising powers, and yet taxes are increasing, the only explanation is that taxes would be *even higher* were it not for the beneficial effects of tax competition. For taxpayers this is a sobering thought.

Tax competition brings opportunities for the UK

The UK has much to gain from tax competition:

- Our moves in the 1980s towards simplified tax structures with low rates (although partially reversed in recent years) put us in a good position to benefit from tax competition when compared with other European countries that combine high tax rates on successful businesses with handouts for failures.
- Our international outlook, geographical position and the

legacy of a relatively low-regulation (in an EU context) business economy mean that in an efficient global capital market the UK would be a natural recipient of capital investment (the UK already receives the lion's share of foreign investment in Europe). If tax competition and low-tax jurisdictions increase the pool of available investment capital and make global capital markets more efficient at distributing it to the most beneficial investments, then the UK is (or could easily put itself) in an ideal position to benefit from this.

- The close historical and constitutional ties, and the common legal framework, that the UK shares with many low-tax jurisdictions are also valuable. They make the UK a natural home for the investment capital that flows through these countries, but also provide wealth through valuable ancillary finance and legal jobs in London. In a time of increasing globalisation the UK should be strengthening these ties, not weakening them by siding with European competitors in attacking our friends.

The UK is therefore in a very strong position to benefit from tax competition, and so we should be supporting it against the attempts of the OECD and the EU to restrict it, while positioning our economy to better reap the benefits.

Tax competition, like other aspects of globalisation, is a fact of modern life, and one that brings great benefits to all society and not just those who directly take advantage of it. But the greatest benefits go to those countries that work in harmony with global free markets, whether in trade, investment or labour, not to those protectionists who try to erect barriers against the tide.

A policy agenda for the UK

If the UK is well placed to benefit from tax competition, what action should its government take to maximise these positive effects? There are several clear policy objectives that need to be followed to ensure that tax competition remains an opportunity, not a threat.

Redirect the focus of the initiatives against tax competition

The obvious approach is to resist further moves towards restrictions on tax competition.

The UK (with Luxembourg) vetoed the EU Savings Tax Directive and delayed its implementation for some time, although finally the nature of EU negotiations saw the UK extract concessions (limiting its negative impact on the City) but give way on the principle. Within the EU resistance may therefore be difficult, although in the wider OECD (and even more so in the UN) there will be more allies to support a principled stance against global tax harmonisation.

Mere resistance can be portrayed as too negative, however, so what is needed is rather a positive approach to strengthen the beneficial aspects of the various initiatives.

Within the EU, the UK has seen some positive results from the tax competition package. The code of conduct group, chaired by the UK, has sought to restrict and eventually eliminate the genuinely harmful 'corporate welfare' aspects of many countries' tax systems. This type of action, against the distortionary special tax breaks for favoured industries that are based on the principle that the government knows best where to direct investment, will strengthen the global economy and favour genuinely productive companies.

The same approach can be adopted in the OECD. The OECD initiative has two parts: action against non-members, and encouragement for members to dismantle their own special tax regimes. As it is generally the OECD members' tax competition (the special tax treatment for particular activities) which is truly harmful, rather than the more general low taxes offered by the classic tax havens, the UK should ensure that this 'internal' cleansing is given at least equal priority. The UK can use its position in the OECD to push for stricter reviews of members' tax regimes, and to ensure that action is not taken against non-members until members' own distortionary tax provisions are dismantled.

This would not be a disguised attempt to block further action against tax competition, but a genuine attempt to improve the global economy by removing distortions. It would also fit well with the UK's general approach to taxation; since the early 1980s the UK has pursued a 'low rate, broad base' approach, where specific tax exemptions and allowances are removed and replaced by the more liberal principle of treating all business decisions alike.

Strengthen other international tax measures

As a related matter, there is much that global bodies could be doing to help rather than hinder the development of the global economy. We have already seen the problems of cross-border investment, with the danger of double or triple taxation, particularly in cross-border investment by private individuals and the mutual funds that serve them. The OECD's approach is still stuck in the past, concentrating on removing double taxation for large-scale corporate foreign direct investment (companies setting up subsidiaries or joint ventures in other countries), and it needs to be reviewed to encourage the modern trend of cross-border 'retail' investment funds.

A host of other minor reforms would also help smooth the global capital markets. Examples would include a better harmonisation of residency rules to prevent dual residence (and hence double taxation), and a more efficient use of mutual agreement procedures. These latter are designed to prevent double taxation when one country objects to a group's transfer pricing policy, by ensuring that both countries party to the transaction calculate taxable profits by using the same price; unfortunately many tax authorities put a low priority on such mechanisms, as they do not see double taxation as being harmful.

If the UK can divert the OECD, and the EU within its borders, to tackle these and related issues, then it will strengthen international capital markets and remove many of the current tax distortions. It is surely a better approach to remove the need to locate investment funds in tax havens rather than attempt to close down the havens without first creating a suitable alternative structure.

This approach would not be a radical departure for either the OECD or the EU, but would instead be strengthening and taking forward their existing work. The OECD already has a good record of reducing double taxation through its tax treaties, and within the EU this would be part of the vital task of extending the single market into the field of private investment.

Further work of this kind would be valuable not only for taxes on capital but also for VAT, where there is much scope for closer international agreement to prevent double taxation through partial application of the source and destination principles. In addition there is a great need within the EU for simplification of VAT administration, which would reduce the compliance problems seen with electronic commerce and other cross-border trading.

Put our own house in order

As part of this strand, the UK should continue to critically examine its own tax system, and remove distortionary elements. There should initially be an end to further 'targeted' tax breaks for particular industries and allowances for special types of investment, following which existing elements should be reviewed and removed. An obvious way forward is to repeal most of the corporate taxation legislation, with its special rules and allowances, and move towards taxing companies on their accounting profits (this has already been a subject of Treasury investigation). Other areas to cover would be the current problems of different levels of tax for incorporated and unincorporated businesses, and the potential double taxation (reduced, but still present) for shareholders, whose dividends are taxed without always giving adequate credit for the fact that they are paid out of profits that have already been taxed at the company level. A similar issue arises with capital gains tax. When taxed profits are retained by a company, other things being equal, it should cause the share price to rise, leading to a potential capital gain on sale and effective double taxation.

These tax reforms may involve a move to a flat tax, with a general abolition of special tax treatments and a full harmonisation of our own internal tax system, or there could be a more incremental approach. Either way, such a reform would be both beneficial in itself (teaching the government to stop backing losers) and would set an example and allow the UK to assume a leadership role in international discussions.

Looking farther, the UK needs to position itself to take advantage of tax competition. In the 1980s the UK led the way in reducing its tax rates, but other countries have matched and even overtaken us and we are falling behind. Reform is needed to ensure that, in a globalised economy, investment capital is not over-taxed in the UK. In part the abolition of special tax treatments would help this: it is estimated that, if companies were taxed on their accounting profits rather than under special tax rules, their tax rate could be reduced from 30 per cent to 23 per cent (Devereaux et al., 2002). Ideally, however, this reform would go farther, positioning the UK as a general low-tax and low-regulation environment.

Promote ties with other jurisdictions

These suggestions would see the UK taking more of a leading role in the various international initiatives, seeing in them the potential for benefits rather than problems. As part of this enhanced role the UK should strengthen its ties with other jurisdictions, particularly those with which it has constitutional, cultural and historical links. These relationships have been damaged by the UK's past negative attitude to tax competition, particularly the Treasury's attempts to enforce the EU savings directive in the Caribbean, and some rebuilding is necessary.

The UK has much to gain from such close links. With strong efforts to improve the taxation of cross-border investment, it is likely that investment funds will continue to need to be located in tax-free jurisdictions for some time, and the UK is well placed to benefit from both their capital flows and their need for professional management.

These suggested approaches are not individual actions,

but part of a wider approach that embraces global markets and seeks to position the UK to best benefit from them. By redirecting the international bodies towards strengthening, rather than damaging, international markets, we strengthen the global economy. By improving our own tax system, the UK positions itself to take best advantage of this improvement, and by reconnecting with other jurisdictions we can also remove some of the non-tax barriers to inbound investment. Finally, closer links with such jurisdictions would enhance the UK's position in multinational bodies, giving it a greater natural role in leading those bodies towards a consensus in favour of tax competition and against the tax cartel of governments, which has the potential to do great damage to economic freedom and prosperity.

REFERENCES

Antigua and Barbuda, Government of (2002), 'Commitment of Antigua and Barbuda', Letter from the prime minister of Antigua and Barbuda to the secretary-general of the OECD, 20 February.

Arthur, T. (2003), 'Tax and the division of labour', *Economic Affairs*, London: Institute of Economic Affairs, March.

Azzara, T. (2003), *Tax Havens of the World*, 8th edn, Copenhagen: Carlton Press.

Baldwin, R. and R. Forslid (2002), 'Tax competition and the nature of capital', Working Papers in Economics, 18, Stockholm University.

Bank for International Settlements (2002), 'Triennial central bank survey of foreign exchange and derivatives market activity 2001 – final results', Basle: BIS, 18 March.

Bartholomew, J. (2004), *The Welfare State We're In*, London: Politico's.

Basnett, F. (1965), *Travels of a Capitalist Lackey*, London: Unwin.

Bassanini, A. and S. Scarpetta (2001), 'The driving forces of economic growth: panel data evidence for the OECD countries', OECD Economic Studies, 33, Paris: OECD.

Benn, E. (1925), *The Confessions of a Capitalist*, London: Benn.

Bennett, A. (2004), 'Battle looms over move to tie US funding for OECD to halt of tax harmonization effort', Washington, DC: Bureau of National Affairs, 12 November.

Bennhold, K. (2004), 'French Socialist links vote on EU Constitution to loss of jobs', *International Herald Tribune*, 10 September.

Boadway, R., K. Cuff and N. Marceau (1999), 'Inter-jurisdictional competition for firms: jobs as vehicles for redistribution', University of Quebec.

Bos, W. (2000), 'Harmful tax competition', Speech to the OECD, Dutch Finance Ministry, 29 June.

Boss, A. (1999), 'Do we need tax harmonisation in the EU?', Kiel Institute of World Economics Working Papers.

Bracewell-Milnes, B. (1976), 'A liberal tax policy: tax neutrality and freedom of choice', *British Tax Review*, 2.

Bracewell-Milnes, B. (1999), 'Tax competition: harmful or beneficial', *Intertax*, 27: 86–8.

Brennan, G. and J. Buchanan (1980), *The Power to Tax: Analytical Foundations of a Fiscal Constitution*, New York: Cambridge University Press.

Brown, G. (2001), '2001 pre-Budget report to the House of Commons', Hansard, 28 November.

Brown, G. (2003), '2003 Budget report to the House of Commons', Hansard, 9 November.

Caplan, B. (1999), 'Standing Tiebout on his head: tax capitalization and the monopoly power of local governments', Independent Institute Working Paper no. 6.

Carnaghan, R. and B. Bracewell-Milnes (1993), *Testing the Market: Competitive Tendering for Government Services in Britain and Abroad*, London: Institute of Economic Affairs.

Clark, A. (1993), *Diaries*, London: Weidenfeld & Nicolson.

Crafts, N. (2002), *Britain's Relative Economic Performance, 1870–1999*, London: Institute of Economic Affairs, London.

Customs Associates Ltd, for the European Commission (2001), 'Study on the competition between alcoholic drinks', Brussels, February.

Dehejia, V. and P. Genschel (1998), 'Tax competition in the European Union', Max-Planck-Institut für Gesellschaftsforschung Discussion Paper 98/3.

Devereaux, M., R. Griffith and A. Klemm (2002), 'Corporate income tax reforms and international tax competition', *Economic Policy*, 35: 451–95.

Edwards, C. and T. DeHaven (2003), 'Corporate welfare', *Cato Handbook for Congress*, Washington, DC: Cato Institute, ch. 33.

Edwards, C. and V. de Rugy (2002), *International Tax Competition: A 21st Century Restraint on Government*, Washington, DC: Cato Institute.

Edwards, J. and M. Keen (1996), 'Tax competition and Leviathan', *European Economic Review*, pp. 113–34.

Eggert, W. (1999), 'Capital tax competition with inefficient government spending', Centre of Finance and Econometrics Discussion Paper, Konstanz University.

EU (European Commission) (2001), 'Report from the Commission on reduced VAT rates', COM(2001) 599 final, Brussels, 22 October.

EU (European Commission) (2003), 'Tax aid – Commission takes stock', IP/03/1605, Brussels, 26 November.

EU (European Commission) (2004a), 'Savings taxation:
Commission welcomes Council agreement on 1 July 2005
application date', Press release, 19 July.

EU (European Commission) (2004b), 'Structures of the taxation
systems in the European Union', Luxembourg.

EU (Eurostat) (2004), 'Total general government revenue (per
cent of GDP)', Brussels.

EU Council of Ministers (1997), 'Resolution on a code of conduct
for business taxation', Brussels, 1 December.

EU Council of Ministers (2001), Memo/01/261, Brussels.

EU Council of Ministers (2002), 'Council Directive 2002/38/
EC on the application of Value Added Tax to electronic
commerce', Brussels.

EU Council of Ministers (2003), 'Council Directive 2003/48/EC
on the taxation of savings income in the form of interest
payments', Brussels, 3 June.

EU Council of Ministers (2004a), 'Council Decision COM
(2004) 75 final on the conclusion of the Agreement between
the European Community and the Swiss Confederation
providing for measures equivalent to those laid down in
Council Directive 2003/48/EC of 3 June 2003 on taxation
of savings income in the form of interest payments and the
accompanying Memorandum of Understanding', Brussels, 10
February.

EU Council of Ministers (2004b), 'Council Decision COM (2004)
455 final on the date of application of Council Directive
2003/48/EC of 3 June 2003 on taxation of savings income in
the form of interest payments', Brussels, 25 June.

EU Council of Ministers (2005), 'Council Decision 2005/25//
EC authorising Denmark to apply a measure derogating

from Article 14(1)(d) of the Sixth Directive 77/388/EC on the harmonisation of laws of the Member States relating to turnover taxes', Brussels, 24 March.

Ganghof, S. (1999), 'Adjusting national tax policy to economic internationalization: strategies and outcomes', Max-Planck-Institut für Gesellschaftsforschung Discussion Paper 99/6.

Genschel, P. (2002), 'Globalisation, tax competition and the welfare state', *Politics and Society*, 30(2), June.

Gorringe, J. (2004), 'UK Foreign Office slams Treasury over EU Savings Tax Directive', Tax-News.com article, 14 May.

Gorter, J. (2000), 'How mobile is capital within the European Union?', Centraal Planbureau (Netherlands Bureau for Economic Policy Analysis), Report 00/4, pp. 23–6.

Gorter, J. and R. Mooij (2001), 'Capital income taxation in Europe: trends and trade-offs', Netherlands Bureau for Economic Policy Analysis.

Greene, G. (1969), *Travels with My Aunt*, London: Bodley Head.

Guardian (2001), 'Dorset One reveals his whereabouts', 17 May.

Gurdgiev, C. (2002), 'Tax competitiveness: can fiscal policy keep up with market demands? Irish proposals for a German tax reform', Brussels: Centre for the New Europe.

Hansard (1999), 'Report of the Treasury Select Committee's examination of witnesses', 2 May.

Hickey, J. (2000), 'The fiscal challenge of E-commerce', *British Tax Review*, 2: 91.

Hong Kong Securities & Futures Commission (1996–2003), 'Net asset value of authorised unit trusts and mutual funds', *Market & Industry Statistics*, Hong Kong.

Hrab, N. (2004), 'Does the European Union believe in ghosts?', *EU Reporter*, 3 May, p. 4.

Huber, B. (2002), 'Tax competition and tax coordination in an optimum income tax model', Economic Policy Research Unit Working Papers.

Hutber, P. (1977), *The Decline and Fall of the Middle Classes*, London: Penguin.

IMF (1997), Annex VI, 'Capital flows to emerging markets – a historical perspective', *International Capital Markets 1997*, Washington, DC: International Monetary Fund.

Janeba, E. (1995), 'Corporate income tax competition, double taxation treaties and foreign direct investment', *Journal of Public Economics*.

Janeba, E. and G. Schjelderup (2004), 'Why Europe should love tax competition – and the US even more so', National Bureau of Economic Research Discussion Paper 23/04.

Johnsson, R. (2004), 'Taxation and domestic free trade – the Ricardian revolution', Austrian Scholars' Conference and Ratio Institute, Stockholm.

Larkins, E. (2001), 'Double tax relief for foreign income: a comparative study of advanced economies', ATAX Discussion Paper no. 4, Sydney: University of New South Wales, June.

Lawson, N. (1992), *The View from No. 11*, London: Bantam Press.

Leach, G. (2003), 'The negative impact of taxation on economic growth', *Reform*, September.

Loungani, P. (2004), *Globalisation without Tears*, Los Angeles, CA: Reason.

McMahon, F. (2001), *A Global Tax: Unworkable, unnecessary and dangerous*, New York: United Nations.

Maddison, A. (2003), *The World Economy: A Millennial Perspective*, Paris: OECD.

Mattingley, M. et al. (2002), 'Report on financial privacy, law enforcement and terrorism', Task Force on Information Exchange and Financial Privacy, Alexandria, VA: Prosperity Institute.

Mitchell, D. (2001), 'A tax competition primer: why tax competition and information exchange undermine America's advantage in the global economy', Washington, DC: Heritage Foundation.

Observer (2002), 'One step ahead of the taxman, and it's legal', 24 February.

OECD (1998), 'Harmful tax competition: an emerging global issue' the '1998 report'), Paris: Organisation for Economic Cooperation and Development.

OECD (2000), 'Towards global tax co-operation: report to the 2000 Ministerial Council Meeting and recommendations by the Committee on Fiscal Affairs: progress in identifying and eliminating harmful tax practices' (the '2000 report'), Paris: Organisation for Economic Cooperation and Development.

OECD (2001a), 'The OECD's project on harmful tax practices: the 2001 progress report' (the '2001 report'), Paris: Organisation for Economic Cooperation and Development.

OECD (2001b), 'OECD says Barbados will not appear on its forthcoming list of uncooperative tax havens', joint OECD and Barbados press release, 31 January.

OECD (2001c), 'Social expenditures 2000', Paris: Organisation for Economic Cooperation and Development.

OECD (2002a), 'The Committee welcomes the progress made in taking forward the review of potentially harmful preferential tax regimes in Member countries', OECD statement by G.

Maklouf, chair of the OECD Committee on Fiscal Affairs, 31 January.

OECD (2002b), 'Offshore financial centres commit to co-operate with OECD to eliminate harmful tax practices', OECD statement, 28 February.

OECD (2002c), 'The OECD issues the list of unco-operative tax havens', Press release, 18 April.

OECD (2004a), 'The OECD's project on harmful tax practices: the 2004 progress report' (the '2004 report'), Paris: Organisation for Economic Cooperation and Development.

OECD (2004b), 'A process for achieving a global level playing field', Paris: Organisation for Economic Cooperation and Development, 4 June.

OECD (2004c), 'OECD in figures, 2004', Paris: Organisation for Economic Cooperation and Development.

OECD (2004d), 'Revenue statistics 1965–2003', Paris: Organisation for Economic Cooperation and Development.

Parkinson, C. (1958), *Parkinson's Law*, London: John Murray.

Parry, I. (2001), 'How large are the welfare costs of tax competition?', Resources for the Future Discussion Paper 01–28, Washington, DC, June.

Patterson, B. and A. Serrano (1998), 'Tax competition in the European Union', European Parliament Working Paper, Economic Affairs Series ECON-105 EN.

Perroni, C. and K. Scharf (1996), 'Tiebout with politics: capital tax competition and constitutional choices', *Review of Economic Studies*, 68: 133–54.

Pinto, C. (1999), '(Harmful) tax competition within the European Union: concept and overview of certain tax regimes in selected Member States', University of Amsterdam.

Primarolo Group (1999), Report of the Code of Conduct group on business taxation (established further to the ECOFIN conclusions of 1 December 1997 on the so-called 'tax-package'), as submitted to the ECOFIN Council, 29 November.

Ratzinger, J. (1984), '*Libertatis nuntius* – instruction on certain aspects of the theology of liberation', Rome: Sacred Congregation for the Doctrine of the Faith, Rome.

Ruding, O. (1992), 'Report of the committee of independent experts on company taxation', Commission of the European Communities, March.

Sabato, Y. (2001), 'How taxes keep high-tech investors away from Israel', Jerusalem: Institute for Advanced Strategic and Political Studies, November.

Smith, A. (1776), *The Wealth of Nations*, Edinburgh.

Sunday Times (2004), 'Rich list', 18 April.

Tanzi, V. and L. Schuknecht (2000), *Public Spending in the 20th Century: A Global Perspective*, Cambridge and New York: Cambridge University Press.

Teather, R. (2002), 'Harmful tax competition?', *Economic Affairs*, London: Institute for Economic Affairs, December.

Tiebout, C. (1956), 'A pure theory of local expenditures', *Journal of Political Economy*, 64: 416–24.

Tullock, G., A. Seldon and G. Brady (2000), *Government: Whose Obedient Servant?*, Readings 51, London: Institute of Economic Affairs.

UK Government (1999), 'Electronic commerce – the UK's taxation agenda', London: HM Customs & Excise/Inland Revenue.

UN (2001), 'Report of the High-Level Panel on Financing for Development', A/55/1000, New York: United Nations.

UN (2003), Fifty-eighth General Assembly, Second Committee, Panel Discussion on 'International cooperation in tax matters', 'Multilateral approach: the best way to tackle capital flight and tax evasion', Press release GA/EF/3048, New York: United Nations, 21 October.

US Census Bureau (2004), 'US trade in goods and services – balance of payments, 1960 thru 2003', Washington, DC: US Census Bureau, Foreign Trade Division, 14 June.

Vanuatu (Government of the Republic of) (2003), Letter of minister of finance and economic development to OECD secretary-general, 7 May.

Wilson, J. (1986), 'A theory of interregional tax competition', *Journal of Urban Economics*, 19: 296–315.

Wilson, J. (1991), 'Tax competition with interregional differences in factor endowments', *Regional Science and Urban Economics*, 21: 423–52.

Wilson, J. (1999), 'Theories of tax competition', *National Tax Journal*, 52(2): 269–304.

World Bank (2004), *World Development Indicators*, Washington, DC: World Bank, April.

WTO (1998), 'France – certain income tax measures constituting subsidies – request for consultations by the United States', Geneva: World Trade Organization, 11 May.

WTO (2002), 'United States – tax treatment for foreign sales corporations – recourse to Article 21.5 of the DSU by the European Communities – AB-2001-8 – report of the Appellate Body', Geneva: World Trade Organization, 14 January.

WTO (2003), 'Merchandise trade by product, region and major trading partner, 2000–02 – United States', Geneva: World Trade Organization.

Zodrow, G. and P. Mieszkowski (1986), 'Pigou, Tiebout, property taxation and the underprovision of local public goods', *Journal of Urban Economics*, 19: 356–70.

ABOUT THE IEA

The Institute is a research and educational charity (No. CC 235 351), limited by guarantee. Its mission is to improve understanding of the fundamental institutions of a free society with particular reference to the role of markets in solving economic and social problems.

The IEA achieves its mission by:

- a high-quality publishing programme
- conferences, seminars, lectures and other events
- outreach to school and college students
- brokering media introductions and appearances

The IEA, which was established in 1955 by the late Sir Antony Fisher, is an educational charity, not a political organisation. It is independent of any political party or group and does not carry on activities intended to affect support for any political party or candidate in any election or referendum, or at any other time. It is financed by sales of publications, conference fees and voluntary donations.

In addition to its main series of publications the IEA also publishes a quarterly journal, *Economic Affairs*.

The IEA is aided in its work by a distinguished international Academic Advisory Council and an eminent panel of Honorary Fellows. Together with other academics, they review prospective IEA publications, their comments being passed on anonymously to authors. All IEA papers are therefore subject to the same rigorous independent refereeing process as used by leading academic journals.

IEA publications enjoy widespread classroom use and course adoptions in schools and universities. They are also sold throughout the world and often translated/reprinted.

Since 1974 the IEA has helped to create a world-wide network of 100 similar institutions in over 70 countries. They are all independent but share the IEA's mission.

Views expressed in the IEA's publications are those of the authors, not those of the Institute (which has no corporate view), its Managing Trustees, Academic Advisory Council members or senior staff.

Members of the Institute's Academic Advisory Council, Honorary Fellows, Trustees and Staff are listed on the following page.

The Institute gratefully acknowledges financial support for its publications programme and other work from a generous benefaction by the late Alec and Beryl Warren.

Other papers recently published by the IEA include:

WHO, What and Why?

Transnational Government, Legitimacy and the World Health Organization
Roger Scruton
Occasional Paper 113; ISBN 0 255 36487 3
£8.00

The World Turned Rightside Up

A New Trading Agenda for the Age of Globalisation
John C. Hulsman
Occasional Paper 114; ISBN 0 255 36495 4
£8.00

The Representation of Business in English Literature

Introduced and edited by Arthur Pollard
Readings 53; ISBN 0 255 36491 1
£12.00

Anti-Liberalism 2000

The Rise of New Millennium Collectivism
David Henderson
Occasional Paper 115; ISBN 0 255 36497 0
£7.50

Capitalism, Morality and Markets

Brian Griffiths, Robert A. Sirico, Norman Barry & Frank Field
Readings 54; ISBN 0 255 36496 2
£7.50

A Conversation with Harris and Seldon

Ralph Harris & Arthur Seldon
Occasional Paper 116; ISBN 0 255 36498 9
£7.50

Malaria and the DDT Story

Richard Tren & Roger Bate
Occasional Paper 117; ISBN 0 255 36499 7
£10.00

A Plea to Economists Who Favour Liberty: Assist the Everyman

Daniel B. Klein
Occasional Paper 118; ISBN 0 255 36501 2
£10.00

The Changing Fortunes of Economic Liberalism

Yesterday, Today and Tomorrow
David Henderson
Occasional Paper 105 (new edition); ISBN 0 255 36520 9
£12.50

The Global Education Industry

Lessons from Private Education in Developing Countries
James Tooley
Hobart Paper 141 (new edition); ISBN 0 255 36503 9
£12.50

Saving Our Streams

The Role of the Anglers' Conservation Association in
Protecting English and Welsh Rivers
Roger Bate
Research Monograph 53; ISBN 0 255 36494 6
£10.00

Better Off Out?

The Benefits or Costs of EU Membership
Brian Hindley & Martin Howe
Occasional Paper 99 (new edition); ISBN 0 255 36502 0
£10.00

Buckingham at 25

Freeing the Universities from State Control
Edited by James Tooley
Readings 55; ISBN 0 255 36512 8
£15.00

Lectures on Regulatory and Competition Policy

Irwin M. Stelzer
Occasional Paper 120; ISBN 0 255 36511 X
£12.50

Misguided Virtue

False Notions of Corporate Social Responsibility
David Henderson
Hobart Paper 142; ISBN 0 255 36510 1
£12.50

HIV and Aids in Schools

The Political Economy of Pressure Groups and Miseducation
Barrie Craven, Pauline Dixon, Gordon Stewart & James Tooley
Occasional Paper 121; ISBN 0 255 36522 5
£10.00

The Road to Serfdom

The Reader's Digest *condensed version*
Friedrich A. Hayek
Occasional Paper 122; ISBN 0 255 36530 6
£7.50

Bastiat's *The Law*

Introduction by Norman Barry
Occasional Paper 123; ISBN 0 255 36509 8
£7.50

A Globalist Manifesto for Public Policy

Charles Calomiris
Occasional Paper 124; ISBN 0 255 36525 X
£7.50

Euthanasia for Death Duties

Putting Inheritance Tax Out of Its Misery
Barry Bracewell-Milnes
Research Monograph 54; ISBN 0 255 36513 6
£10.00

Liberating the Land

The Case for Private Land-use Planning
Mark Pennington
Hobart Paper 143; ISBN 0 255 36508 x
£10.00

IEA Yearbook of Government Performance 2002/2003

Edited by Peter Warburton
Yearbook 1; ISBN 0 255 36532 2
£15.00

Britain's Relative Economic Performance, 1870– 1999

Nicholas Crafts
Research Monograph 55; ISBN 0 255 36524 1
£10.00

Should We Have Faith in Central Banks?

Otmar Issing
Occasional Paper 125; ISBN 0 255 36528 4
£7.50

The Dilemma of Democracy

Arthur Seldon
Hobart Paper 136 (reissue); ISBN 0 255 36536 5
£10.00

Capital Controls: a 'Cure' Worse Than the Problem?

Forrest Capie

Research Monograph 56; ISBN 0 255 36506 3

£10.00

The Poverty of 'Development Economics'

Deepak Lal

Hobart Paper 144 (reissue); ISBN 0 255 36519 5

£15.00

Should Britain Join the Euro?

The Chancellor's Five Tests Examined

Patrick Minford

Occasional Paper 126; ISBN 0 255 36527 6

£7.50

Post-Communist Transition: Some Lessons

Leszek Balcerowicz

Occasional Paper 127; ISBN 0 255 36533 0

£7.50

A Tribute to Peter Bauer

John Blundell et al.

Occasional Paper 128; ISBN 0 255 36531 4

£10.00

Employment Tribunals

Their Growth and the Case for Radical Reform

J. R. Shackleton

Hobart Paper 145; ISBN 0 255 36515 2

£10.00

Fifty Economic Fallacies Exposed

Geoffrey E. Wood
Occasional Paper 129; ISBN 0 255 36518 7
£12.50

A Market in Airport Slots

Keith Boyfield (editor), David Starkie, Tom Bass & Barry Humphreys
Readings 56; ISBN 0 255 36505 5
£10.00

Money, Inflation and the Constitutional Position of the Central Bank

Milton Friedman & Charles A. E. Goodhart
Readings 57; ISBN 0 255 36538 1
£10.00

railway.com

Parallels between the Early British Railways and the ICT Revolution
Robert C. B. Miller
Research Monograph 57; ISBN 0 255 36534 9
£12.50

The Regulation of Financial Markets

Edited by Philip Booth & David Currie
Readings 58; ISBN 0 255 36551 9
£12.50

Climate Alarmism Reconsidered
Robert L. Bradley Jr
Hobart Paper 146; ISBN 0 255 36541 1
£12.50

Government Failure: E. G. West on Education
Edited by James Tooley & James Stanfield
Occasional Paper 130; ISBN 0 255 36552 7
£12.50

Waging the War of Ideas
John Blundell
Second edition
Occasional Paper 131; ISBN 0 255 36547 0
£12.50

Corporate Governance: Accountability in the Marketplace
Elaine Sternberg
Second edition
Hobart Paper 147; ISBN 0 255 36542 X
£12.50

The Land Use Planning System
Evaluating Options for Reform
John Corkindale
Hobart Paper 148; ISBN 0 255 36550 0
£10.00

Economy and Virtue

Essays on the Theme of Markets and Morality
Edited by Dennis O'Keeffe
Readings 59; ISBN 0 255 36504 7
£12.50

Free Markets Under Siege

Cartels, Politics and Social Welfare
Richard A. Epstein
Occasional Paper 132; ISBN 0 255 36553 5
£10.00

Unshackling Accountants

D. R. Myddelton
Hobart Paper 149; ISBN 0 255 36559 4
£12.50

The Euro as Politics

Pedro Schwartz
Research Monograph 58; ISBN 0 255 36535 7
£12.50

Pricing Our Roads

Vision and Reality
Stephen Glaister & Daniel J. Graham
Research Monograph 59; ISBN 0 255 36562 4
£10.00

The Role of Business in the Modern World

Progress, Pressures, and Prospects for the Market Economy

David Henderson

Hobart Paper 150; ISBN 0 255 36548 9

£12.50

Public Service Broadcasting Without the BBC?

Alan Peacock

Occasional Paper 133; ISBN 0 255 36565 9

£10.00

The ECB and the Euro: the First Five Years

Otmar Issing

Occasional Paper 134; ISBN 0 255 36555 1

£10.00

Towards a Liberal Utopia?

Edited by Philip Booth

Hobart Paperback 32; ISBN 0 255 36563 2

£15.00

The Way Out of the Pensions Quagmire

Philip Booth & Deborah Cooper

Research Monograph 60; ISBN 0 255 36517 9

£12.50

Black Wednesday

A Re-examination of Britain's Experience in the Exchange Rate Mechanism

Alan Budd

Occasional Paper 135; ISBN 0 255 36566 7

£7.50

Crime: Economic Incentives and Social Networks
Paul Ormerod
Hobart Paper 151; ISBN 0 255 36554 3
£10.00

The Road to Serfdom *with* The Intellectuals and Socialism
Friedrich A. Hayek
Occasional Paper 136; ISBN 0 255 36576 4
£10.00

Money and Asset Prices in Boom and Bust
Tim Congdon
Hobart Paper 152; ISBN 0 255 36570 5
£10.00

The Dangers of Bus Re-regulation
and Other Perspectives on Markets in Transport
John Hibbs et al.
Occasional Paper 137; ISBN 0 255 36572 1
£10.00

The New Rural Economy
Change, Dynamism and Government Policy
Berkeley Hill et al.
Occasional Paper 138; ISBN 0 255 36546 2
£15.00

To order copies of currently available IEA papers, or to enquire about availability, please contact:

Gazelle
IEA orders
FREEPOST RLYS-EAHU-YSCZ
White Cross Mills
Hightown
Lancaster LA1 4XS

Tel: 01524 68765
Fax: 01524 63232
Email: sales@gazellebooks.co.uk

The IEA also offers a subscription service to its publications. For a single annual payment, currently £40.00 in the UK, you will receive every monograph the IEA publishes during the course of a year and discounts on our extensive back catalogue. For more information, please contact:

Adam Myers
Subscriptions
The Institute of Economic Affairs
2 Lord North Street
London SW1P 3LB

Tel: 020 7799 8920
Fax: 020 7799 2137
Website: www.iea.org.uk